Holiday SLOW COOKER

Holiday SLOW COOKER

100 Incredible & Festive Recipes for Every Celebration

LEIGH ANNE WILKES founder of Your Homebased Mom

PAGE STREET
PUBLISHING CO.

PAGE STREET
PUBLISHING CO.

First published in 2017 by

Page Street Publishing Co.

27 Congress Street, Suite 105

Salem, MA 01970

www.pagestreetpublishing.com

Distributed by Macmillan, sales in Canada by The Canadian Manda Group.

21 20 19 18 17   1 2 3 4 5

ISBN-13: 978-1-62414-419-6

ISBN-10: 1-62414-419-5

Library of Congress Control Number: 2017937059

Cover and book design by Page Street Publishing Co.

Photography by Erica Allen

Printed and bound in China

DEDICATION

To my family: Jim, Logan & Ashley, Clark & Jessica, Cali & Tessa.
Thank you for loving food as much as I do and for loving me.

CONTENTS

INTRODUCTION

Welcome to my kitchen. The crackling of oil in a hot pan, the fragrant scent of a tri-tip in the slow cooker, that decadent first bite of a warm cookie—these are the sounds, smells and tastes that have brought my family and friends together throughout the years. From holiday celebrations to neighborhood gatherings to taking meals to a new mother and everything in between, food is what binds and comforts us. It's by standing side by side at the counter, mixing, dipping, dicing, tasting and stirring that we have created some of our most favorite and lasting memories. My hope is that with the *Holiday Slow Cooker* cookbook, you can likewise create delicious food and lasting memories for and with the people you care about most.

In this book, you will find recipes that wow—perfect for special occasions and everyday use, too. I think you'll find that these recipes will come to be family favorites that you will use over and over again, regardless of season, and always to rave reviews.

Maybe you're like me—late to discover the benefits of using a slow cooker, only dusting it off every now and then for the occasional Sunday pot roast. I have my blog readers to thank for the permanent place my slow cooker (ok, slow cookers, I may or may not own four of them . . .) has in my kitchen. About ten years ago, at the advent of my blog, Your Homebased Mom, readers began requesting slow cooker recipes. The recipes I shared ended up being some of my most popular recipes on the blog. I now use my slow cookers multiple times a week, and it's not uncommon to see two or three running at the same time on my countertop.

Oh, how I wish I had appreciated and used my slow cooker more when my children were younger. Learn from my mistake! It would have made my life so much easier. Here's why:

· Less mess: With a slow cooker, there are fewer dishes to wash (you can thank me later).

· Amazing aromas: My house always smells amazing when a slow cooker is working away, doing its thing in my kitchen.

· Low maintenance: While that slow cooker is working, I can be off doing something else!

· Double trouble: For years, I dreamed of having a second oven. Little did I know that I had one sitting on a shelf in the back of my coat closet! Your slow cooker is just as good as a second oven—stick with me throughout this cookbook, and I'll show you why.

Not convinced yet? Let me tell you what's on the menu. Not only is there a lovely pot roast recipe included, but you will also find recipes for dozens of delicious main dishes, sides, desserts, beverages, breakfast foods and brunch treats. A slow cooker can pretty much cook anything your oven can! When you're sufficiently obsessed with these 100 slow cooker recipes (as I know you will be), head over to yourhomebasedmom.com for dozens more delicious, family-friendly slow cooker recipes.

My hope is that this cookbook will facilitate gatherings with the people you love, help you cook delicious food and make your life easier, especially during the holiday season. So get that slow cooker out of the closet, plug it in and make it a regular part of your weekly meal planning.

Leigh Anne Wilkes

THANKSGIVING

Thanksgiving is one of my favorite holidays and my favorite holiday meal to prepare, but it can also be a challenge to get everything finished at the same time and on the table. Whether we have a crowd (50 extended family members or more) or it's just our immediate family (8 people), using the slow cooker can make a huge difference in the kitchen and in my ability to get our Thanksgiving meal on the table. If you have a smaller crowd, putting the Herbed Turkey Breast (page 12) in the slow cooker will free up your oven for all the sides. I also like to prepare my sides in the slow cooker. In fact, my husband prefers my Sausage Cornbread Dressing (page 17) done in the slow cooker rather than in the oven!

If you are feeding a larger crowd, put the turkey in the oven and line up the slow cookers for all the sides, including Pecan and Brown Sugar Sweet Potatoes (page 15), Not Your Grandmother's Creamed Corn (page 20), Creamy Simple Mashed Potatoes (page 14) and even the rolls. The Garlic Cheese Rolls (page 24) are a family favorite!

And don't forget dessert. Pumpkin pie lovers are going to love the Spiced Pumpkin Pudding Cake (page 19), especially with a scoop of vanilla ice cream.

HERBED TURKEY BREAST

When you have a smaller crowd to feed for the holidays, a turkey breast is the way to go.
The herb butter rub keeps the turkey moist and so flavorful. Using the slow cooker frees up
your oven space for all the Thanksgiving side dishes.

SERVES 4 TO 6

2 tbsp (29 g) butter, softened

½ tsp dried basil

½ tsp dried thyme leaves

½ tsp garlic powder

½ tsp sea salt

¼ tsp pepper

3 lb (1.5 kg) turkey breast, with bone and skin

¼ cup (60 ml) chicken broth

Mix together the butter, herbs, garlic powder, salt and pepper.

Loosen the skin on the turkey breast and rub the herbed butter mixture between the skin and meat.

Add the chicken broth to a 6-quart (6-L) slow cooker.

Place the turkey breast in the slow cooker and cook on low for 4 to 5 hours or until it reaches 165°F (74°C).

CREAMY SIMPLE MASHED POTATOES

My husband is from Idaho and loves his potatoes. He is a purist when it comes to mashed potatoes. He likes them with just a little butter, salt and pepper. This recipe is simple, just as he likes them, but feel free to dress it up with additional seasonings, cream cheese or sour cream. Also, I have found that Yukon gold potatoes work better than russets. The russets tend to discolor in the slow cooker, and we prefer the texture of the Yukon golds.

SERVES 4 TO 6

3 lb (1.5 kg) Yukon gold potatoes

½ cup (118 ml) chicken broth

1 tsp onion powder

1 tsp garlic powder

2 tbsp (28 g) butter

Milk, as needed

¼ cup (30 g) sour cream, optional

1 tbsp (3 g) herbs of choice, optional

2 tbsp (30 g) cream cheese, optional

Salt and pepper to taste

Peel the potatoes and cut them into quarters.

Put the potatoes, broth, onion powder and garlic powder into a 6-quart (6-L) slow cooker. Cook on high for 3 to 4 hours.

Drain the potatoes (reserve the liquid to add back in if needed) and mash them until smooth. Add the butter and a little milk or potato water to achieve the desired consistency.

At this point, you can dress up the mashed potatoes however you like by adding additional seasonings, cream cheese or sour cream.

PECAN AND BROWN SUGAR SWEET POTATOES

I got this recipe from my husband's aunt years ago, and it quickly became a family favorite. You can make these sweet potatoes in the oven, but I love using my slow cooker so I don't have to worry about them, and I can keep my oven free. You may wonder whether you are eating dinner or dessert when you taste them!

SERVES 8 TO 10

3 lb (1.5 kg) sweet potatoes, peeled and cut into 1-inch (25-mm) cubes

2 cups (473 ml) chicken or vegetable broth

¾ cup (177 ml) orange juice

2 tbsp (18 g) brown sugar

½ tsp salt

1 tsp cinnamon

1 cup (116 g) toasted pecans, chopped

Place the sweet potatoes into a 6-quart (6-L) slow cooker and cover them with the broth. Cook on high for 4 to 5 hours.

Drain the remaining broth from the sweet potatoes and add the orange juice, brown sugar, salt and cinnamon to the sweet potatoes. Use a hand mixer to blend until the sweet potatoes have reached your desired texture.

Place the sweet potatoes into a serving dish, top with the chopped pecans and serve.

SAUSAGE CORNBREAD DRESSING

We have been making this dressing for over 30 years at our house. We can't celebrate Thanksgiving without it. We prefer our dressing on the drier side, but if you prefer your dressing a little wetter, just add more gravy! The addition of sausage gives this dressing a lot of flavor. I love that I can make it in the slow cooker because it frees up my oven for other Thanksgiving goodness.

SERVES 8

16 oz (454 g) regular breakfast sausage

1 cup (151 g) chopped onion

1½ cups (151 g) chopped celery

¼ cup (58 g) butter

1 (12-oz [340-g]) box cornbread dressing

2½ cups (592 ml) chicken broth

1 cup (116 g) pecans, lightly chopped

In a medium-size pan over medium heat, cook the sausage until browned and cooked through, about 5 minutes. Remove into a bowl and in the same pan, sauté the onion and celery in butter over medium heat for about 5 minutes.

Mix together the dressing, browned sausage, onions and celery. Stir in the chicken broth.

Line a 6-quart (6-L) slow cooker with a plastic liner. Add the dressing mixture and cook on low for 3 to 4 hours.

Remove the lid during the last 30 minutes to allow the top to crisp up.

Sprinkle with pecans and serve.

CITRUS CRANBERRY SAUCE

Citrus Cranberry Sauce can easily be made a few days ahead and refrigerated until you are ready to serve it. The use of the slow cooker helps infuse and enhance all the great citrus flavors in this sauce. You can switch up your citrus if you want and add lemon zest in place of the orange zest or add both.

SERVES 8 TO 10

1 lb (454 g) whole fresh cranberries

½ cup (118 ml) freshly squeezed orange juice

½ cup (118 ml) water

½ cup (72 g) brown sugar

½ cup (96 g) granulated sugar

¼ tsp salt

1 orange, zested

1 (20-oz [567-g]) can crushed pineapple, including the juice

Place all the ingredients into a 6-quart (6-L) slow cooker and stir to combine.

Cook on high for 2 to 3 hours and then on low for 4 to 5 hours.

Refrigerate until you are ready to serve it.

APPLE CRISP

This Apple Crisp can also be made with pears, peaches or fresh berries. There is a secret little ingredient in this crisp that gives it some fun extra flavor—graham crackers! Removing the lid during the last hour of cooking will help the topping crisp up.

SERVES 8

4 to 6 Granny Smith apples, peeled, cored and sliced

9 graham cracker sheets (1 sleeve)

¾ cup (165 g) brown sugar, packed

½ cup (40 g) old-fashioned oats

½ cup (63 g) flour

1 tsp cinnamon

½ tsp nutmeg

½ cup (118 g) butter, melted

Place the prepared apples into a 6-quart (6-L) slow cooker.

Finely chop the graham crackers into crumbs. I use my food processor. Combine the crumbs, sugar, oats, flour and spices. Add the butter, mixing well to combine.

Sprinkle the mixture over the apples.

Cook on low for 2 hours. Remove the lid and cook for 1 additional hour.

SPICED PUMPKIN PUDDING CAKE

This Spiced Pumpkin Pudding Cake is the perfect alternative to pumpkin pie—or you could serve both! A delicious sauce forms at the bottom of the slow cooker as a moist cake bakes on top. And it is perfect topped with ice cream or whipped cream.

SERVES 6 TO 8

1½ cups (188 g) flour

1¼ cups (180 g) brown sugar, divided

1 tsp baking powder

1 tsp baking soda

¼ tsp salt

2 tsp (5 g) cinnamon, divided

½ tsp ground cloves

½ tsp ground nutmeg

½ cup (120 ml) pumpkin puree

½ cup (60 g) sour cream

2 tbsp (30 ml) canola oil or melted butter

1 tsp vanilla

2 tbsp (30 ml) hot water

½ cup (60 g) chopped pecans

1½ cups (355 ml) boiling water

Spray the inside of a 6-quart (6-L) slow cooker with nonstick cooking spray.

In a bowl, whisk together the flour, ½ cup (72 g) brown sugar, baking powder, baking soda, salt, 1 teaspoon of cinnamon, cloves and nutmeg. In another bowl, combine the pumpkin, sour cream, oil, vanilla and hot water.

Mix the wet ingredients into the dry ingredients (it should be like thick cookie dough). Spread it evenly onto the bottom of the slow cooker.

Mix ¾ cup (108 g) of brown sugar and 1 teaspoon of cinnamon together with the pecans. Sprinkle it over the top of the batter. Gently pour the boiling water over the top.

Cook on high for 1 to 2 hours. Use a toothpick to check the cake; it should come out clean. The cake will begin to pull away from the sides of the slow cooker.

Spoon into individual bowls, add the sauce that formed on the bottom of the slow cooker and ice cream or whipped cream.

NOT YOUR GRANDMOTHER'S CREAMED CORN

Creamed corn is considered comfort food at our house, and it always reminds my husband of his grandmother. I like this version better than the traditional creamed corn, as you have the texture of whole corn but the creaminess of creamed corn. It is the perfect addition to any holiday menu or a weeknight dinner, too. I like to sprinkle the paprika over the top right before serving with an additional dusting of some Parmesan cheese.

SERVES 8 TO 10

½ cup (115 g) butter

4 oz (113 g) cream cheese

2 (16-oz [454-g]) bags frozen corn, one white and one yellow

½ tsp salt

¼ tsp pepper

½ tsp garlic powder

½ cup (118 ml) whole milk

1 tbsp (12 g) sugar

½ cup (90 g) freshly grated Parmesan cheese

Paprika, for sprinkling on top

Over medium heat, melt the butter and cream cheese in a saucepan on the stovetop until they're combined, about 4 to 5 minutes.

Place the corn, salt, pepper, garlic powder, milk and sugar in a 6-quart (6-L) slow cooker. Stir in the butter and cream cheese mixture.

Cook on high for 1 to 2 hours or on low for 3 to 4 hours.

Stir in the Parmesan cheese 30 minutes before serving. Right before serving, sprinkle the corn with paprika and some additional Parmesan cheese.

TROPICAL BROWN SUGAR CARROTS

These carrots taste a little bit more like candy than a vegetable, thanks to the brown sugar and pineapple. For even cooking, be sure your carrots are cut into pieces around the same size. I like to cut them into 1-inch (25-mm) pieces, but if you want them smaller, simply adjust the cooking time down a bit. I like to use the fork test for tenderness. The fork slides easily into the carrot without the carrot falling apart. Not too mushy, but not too hard.

SERVES 8

2 lb (907 g) carrots, peeled and cut into 1-inch (25-mm) pieces

2 tbsp (29 g) butter

¼ cup (36 g) brown sugar

1 cup (225 g) drained crushed pineapple

⅓ cup (78 ml) pineapple juice

Fresh parsley, for garnish

Place the carrots in a 6-quart (6-L) slow cooker.

In a saucepan over medium heat, melt the butter. Add the brown sugar, pineapple and pineapple juice. Stir to combine, and pour it over the carrots.

Cover and cook on high for 2 to 3 hours or on low for 4 hours. The time may vary depending on the size of your carrots. I like to remove the lid for the last 30 to 40 minutes to allow the carrots to absorb some of the juices in the slow cooker.

Spinkle with fresh parsley for garnish, if desired.

GARLIC CHEESE ROLLS

These rolls are my version of a yummy roll from a favorite restaurant. I was so excited to be able to create these at home and to make them in my slow cooker. I originally made them in the oven but discovered that it is even faster and easier to make them in the slow cooker since I don't need to let the dough thaw and rise for several hours before baking.

SERVES 10

10 frozen dinner rolls

¼ cup (55 g) mayonnaise

¼ cup (57 g) butter, melted

⅓ cup (60 g) freshly grated Parmesan cheese

Garlic powder

Dried parsley

Line a 4-quart (4-L) slow cooker with parchment paper.

Dip a frozen roll into mayonnaise, then butter and, lastly, cheese. Place the roll cheese side up in the slow cooker. Repeat with the remaining rolls.

Sprinkle the rolls with garlic powder and parsley.

Place a cotton towel or paper towel between the slow cooker and the lid to absorb condensation.

Cook on high for 2 hours.

CHRISTMAS

Just like Thanksgiving, Christmas is always a bit of a challenge when it comes to the kitchen and dinner prep. Let your slow cooker help you out whether you use it for the main dish, the sides or even dessert!

We love a good roast at our house for Christmas, and the Santa Maria–Style Pot Roast (page 28) is the perfect choice. Serve it with the Roasted Garlic and Herbed Mashed Potatoes (page 39) and the Teriyaki Glazed Brussels Sprouts (page 43), but if your family prefers turkey, try the Herbed Turkey Breast (page 12). If you do a lot of entertaining during the holidays, you will love the Mushroom Artichoke Chicken (page 30), which was always my mother's go-to entertaining recipe while I was growing up. It is perfect served with the Cashew Nut Rice Pilaf (page 67).

The Cranberry Balsamic Pork Loin Roast (page 36) has nice holiday flair to it thanks to the cranberries. I always love to have a slow cooker of Cranberry-Apple-Spiced Cider (page 33) or Creamy Malted Hot Chocolate (page 33) going to help warm up my guests or the kids after they come in from the cold.

SANTA MARIA–STYLE POT ROAST

Santa Maria roast gets its name from a city in California. A Santa Maria rub typically is a mixture of salt, pepper, garlic, parsley and whatever else you want to add to it. It is traditionally done with a tri-tip roast, but it also makes a delicious pot roast. Add some carrots and potatoes, and you've got a perfect pot roast. Feel free to get creative and add additional favorite seasonings, but it really doesn't need it. You will have lots of delicious liquid in the slow cooker that you can use to make gravy if you want.

SERVES 4 TO 6

2 tbsp (30 g) sea salt

1 tsp black pepper

1 tsp garlic powder

1 tsp dried parsley

½ tsp sugar

3 lb (1.5 kg) boneless chuck roast

2 tbsp (29 ml) olive oil

3 carrots, peeled and cut into 1-inch (25-mm) pieces

3 to 4 medium potatoes, peeled and cut in half and then quartered

2 cups (473 ml) beef broth

Mix together the salt, pepper, garlic powder, parsley and sugar and rub over both sides of the roast.

Heat the olive oil in a pan large enough for the pot roast over medium heat, and then sear the roast on both sides for about 3 to 4 minutes or until browned.

Place the carrots and potatoes in a 6-quart (6-L) slow cooker and place the roast on top. Add the beef broth, being careful not to pour it over the top of the roast and wash off the seasonings.

Cook on low for 6 to 8 hours or on high for 3 to 4 hours or until the meat is tender and falling apart.

MUSHROOM ARTICHOKE CHICKEN

During my childhood, Mushroom Artichoke Chicken made an appearance at almost every dinner party my mom hosted. When you find a good recipe, you stick with it! This chicken dish is perfect for company because it looks elegant, tastes delicious and is so easy to make. I adapted it for the slow cooker, making it even easier and freeing up your oven.

SERVES 4

4 boneless, skinless chicken breasts

1 tsp salt

½ tsp pepper

½ tsp smoked paprika

¼ cup (57 g) butter

3 tbsp (23 g) flour

2 cups (473 ml) chicken broth

½ tsp thyme leaves

1 (14-oz [397-g]) jar artichoke hearts, drained and rinsed

½ lb (226 g) mushrooms, trimmed, washed and halved

Season the chicken with salt, pepper and smoked paprika. Melt the butter over medium heat in a large frying pan and add the chicken. Brown until golden on both sides, 3 to 4 minutes each side.

Place the chicken in a 6-quart (6-L) slow cooker.

In the butter that is remaining in the frying pan, add the flour and stir to mix. Add the chicken broth and thyme, and cook until the sauce thickens and has a gravy-like consistency. Add salt and pepper to taste.

Pour the sauce over the chicken and cook on low for 4 hours. During the last hour, add the artichoke hearts and sliced mushrooms.

Serve with Cashew Nut Rice Pilaf (page 67).

CHOCOLATE TOFFEE FONDUE

Fondue on Christmas Eve has been a tradition in our family for over 50 years. It was a childhood tradition for me, and I continued it with my family. This chocolate fondue has a lot of versatility. We love to add toffee bits to it, but you can dress it up however you like with your favorite add-in or flavor extracts. Some peppermint extract and a swirl of marshmallow cream are always fun choices. We love using strawberries, bananas, orange segments, pretzels, marshmallows and pound cake to dip into the fondue.

SERVES 6 TO 8

9 oz (255 g) milk chocolate

9 oz (255 g) dark chocolate

½ cup (148 g) hazelnut spread (we like to use Nutella)

1 cup (236 ml) heavy whipping cream

1 tsp vanilla

½ cup (78 g) toffee bits

Add all of the ingredients except the toffee bits to a 4-quart (4-L) slow cooker and cook on low for 1 hour.

Stir 3 to 4 times until all the chocolate is melted and smooth. Add the toffee bits or other desired mix-ins right before serving.

CRANBERRY–APPLE–SPICED CIDER

This is our favorite beverage during the holiday season. We usually kick off the season with our first batch of cider on Halloween and continue enjoying it through the New Year! I think the longer the cider cooks, the better it tastes.

SERVES 10 TO 12

64 oz (2 L) apple cider

1 cup (236 ml) canned orange juice, reconstituted

1 cup (236 ml) cranberry juice

¼ cup (36 g) brown sugar

4 whole cinnamon sticks

½ tsp whole cloves

½ tsp whole allspice

Place all the ingredients in a 6-quart (6-L) slow cooker and cook on high for 3 to 4 hours or on low for 6 to 8 hours.

CREAMY MALTED HOT CHOCOLATE

The slow cooker is the perfect place to make hot chocolate because you don't need to worry about burning it on the bottom of the pan, which always happens to me. To get creamy hot chocolate, I always use whole milk. The addition of vanilla extract and malt powder makes this hot chocolate the best!

SERVES 4 TO 6

⅔ cup (73 g) unsweetened cocoa

⅔ cup (156 ml) hot water

1 cup (192 g) granulated sugar

Pinch of salt

1 cup (116 g) malted milk powder

2 tsp (10 ml) vanilla

4 cups (946 ml) whole milk

In a 4-quart (4-L) slow cooker, mix the cocoa and hot water together and stir until smooth. This will help prevent the cocoa from becoming lumpy.

Add the sugar, salt, malted milk powder, vanilla and milk, and stir to combine.

Heat on high for 1 hour, and then turn down to low or warm while serving.

FRUIT AND NUT BRIE

Brie is one of my favorite appetizers. This recipe is super versatile, and you can make it your own by selecting your favorite jam or preserve flavor, nuts and herbs. My favorite combination is raspberry, almond and thyme, but I also love peach, pecans and basil. Cooking the Brie in the slow cooker allows the cheese to melt evenly, and you don't have to watch it as closely as you do when it is in the oven. If you have a large slow cooker, place the Brie in an oven-safe container and then inside the slow cooker. With smaller slow cookers, you can place it directly in the slow cooker.

SERVES 4 TO 6

1 (8-oz [227-g]) round of Brie (if you use a larger Brie, increase the amount of the other ingredients accordingly)

¼ cup (80 g) jam or preserves

3 tbsp (32 g) nuts

1 tsp minced fresh herbs

Line a 6-quart (6-L) slow cooker with parchment paper.

Slice through the rind on top of the Brie in a grid pattern. You can also cut the rind off the top if you prefer.

Spread the jam over the top, within ¼ inch (6 mm) of the edge. Sprinkle with the nuts and add the herbs on top.

Place the Brie in the slow cooker. Cook on high for 1 hour or until the cheese is melted through.

CRANBERRY BALSAMIC PORK LOIN ROAST

This Cranberry Balsamic Pork Loin Roast is just the thing for a holiday dinner. It's a great alternative to a beef roast, and the cranberry sauce adds a sweet and festive feel to the pork roast. I like to serve it sliced, so I cook it on high for 4 hours, but if you prefer to be able to shred the meat, cook it longer at low for 8 hours. Thicken up the sauce at the end with some cornstarch and spoon it over the sliced or shredded meat.

SERVES 6 TO 8

1 tbsp (15 ml) olive oil

Salt and pepper to taste

3 to 4 lb (1.5 to 2 kg) boneless pork loin roast

½ cup (76 g) chopped onion

½ cup (118 ml) chicken broth

1 (14-oz [397-g]) can whole berry cranberry sauce, divided

2 tbsp (30 ml) balsamic vinegar

2 tsp (4 g) orange zest

2 tbsp (19 g) cornstarch

Heat the oil in a pan over medium-high heat.

Salt and pepper both sides of the pork roast. Sear the meat on all sides, 2 to 3 minutes each side, and place it in a 6-quart (6-L) slow cooker.

In the pan you used to sear the pork, add the onions, chicken broth and half the can of whole berry cranberry sauce. Stir to mix. Add the balsamic vinegar and orange zest, and pour the sauce over the pork loin.

Cook on high for 4 hours for a sliceable roast or on low for 8 hours to shred the roast.

During the last 30 minutes, remove ½ cup (118 ml) of the juice and add the cornstarch to it. Mix it to dissolve the cornstarch, and then add it back to the slow cooker. Stir to combine, and then allow it to thicken.

Remove the pork loin, cover it with foil and let it rest for 15 minutes.

Add the remaining cranberry sauce to the juices in the slow cooker and stir to combine. If the sauce hasn't thickened enough, add it to a saucepan on the stovetop and bring it to a boil. Reduce the heat and allow it to simmer and thicken, 1 to 2 minutes.

Serve the roast sliced with sauce drizzled over the top.

RED PEPPER AND GREEN BEAN CASSEROLE

Green beans and red pepper make a perfect, colorful and festive combination for Christmas. The beans are garnished with sliced almonds for some added crunch and Parmesan cheese for additional flavor.

SERVES 8 TO 10

2 lb (900 g) frozen cut green beans

1 (10.75-oz [298-g]) can cream of chicken soup

¼ cup (60 ml) whole milk

1 cup (120 g) Monterey Jack cheese

½ tsp onion powder

½ tsp garlic powder

1 tbsp (15 ml) Worcestershire sauce

1 red pepper, diced

½ cup (46 g) toasted sliced almonds, for garnish

½ cup (90 g) freshly grated Parmesan cheese, for garnish

Place the frozen green beans into a 6-quart (6-L) slow cooker.

Combine the soup, milk, Monterey Jack cheese, onion powder, garlic powder, Worcestershire sauce and red pepper, and pour it over the beans.

Cook on low for 5 hours or on high for 2 to 3 hours. Remove the lid during the last 30 minutes to help the gravy thicken up.

Garnish with sliced almonds and Parmesan cheese.

ROASTED GARLIC AND HERB MASHED POTATOES

My husband loves his mashed potatoes. I think they are too much work, all that peeling! This recipe is the perfect compromise for us and keeps my husband happy. No peeling required, and the addition of roasted garlic dresses up these potatoes.

SERVES 8

2 lb (907 g) red potatoes, quartered

1 tsp oregano or Italian seasoning

1 tsp salt

½ tsp pepper

1 head Roasted Garlic (page 40)

½ cup (118 ml) chicken broth

¼ cup (57 g) butter

⅓ cup (78 ml) milk or cream

Spray the inside of a 6-quart (6-L) slow cooker with cooking spray.

Add the potatoes, seasonings, roasted garlic and chicken broth, and cook on low for 3 hours or on high for 1 to 1½ hours.

Use a hand mixer to blend the potatoes.

Add the butter and milk slowly, a little at a time. You may not need the full amount of milk, or you may need additional milk to get the consistency of the potatoes you prefer.

Add more seasonings if needed.

Keep the potatoes warm in the slow cooker until you are ready to serve.

ROASTED GARLIC

Roasting garlic in a slow cooker is a breeze. I like to do a big batch and then refrigerate or freeze what I don't need right away. Roasted Garlic is the perfect addition to so many different dishes, including Roasted Garlic Artichoke Dip (page 169) and Roasted Garlic and Herb Mashed Potatoes (page 39). Once you have it on hand, you will find all kinds of dishes to add it to. I also love to spread it on a fresh baguette!

SERVES 4 TO 5

4 to 5 heads of garlic

2 to 3 tbsp (30 to 44 ml) olive oil

Slice the top off a head of garlic so that the cloves are exposed.

Coat the bottom of a 6-quart (6-L) slow cooker with olive oil, and add the garlic cut side down.

Cook on low for about 4 hours. The garlic will brown slightly and become very soft.

Squeeze the head of garlic to get the garlic out.

TERIYAKI GLAZED BRUSSELS SPROUTS

I fell in love with these Brussels sprouts when I ate a similar version at a local restaurant here in Portland. I knew I had to immediately go home and figure out how to recreate them. The sweetness of the sauce is a perfect match for the Brussels sprouts, and the slow, even cooking of the slow cooker is the perfect way to get them tender.

SERVES 6 TO 8

1½ lb (680 g) Brussels sprouts, trimmed and cut in half lengthwise

2 tbsp (30 ml) olive oil

½ tsp salt

½ tsp pepper

¼ cup (59 ml) soy sauce

¼ cup (55 g) packed brown sugar

1 tbsp (15 ml) rice vinegar

½ tsp fresh ginger, minced

Place the Brussels sprouts in a 6-quart (6-L) slow cooker.

Drizzle them with oil, salt and pepper. Toss to coat.

Cook on low for 3 hours or on high for 1½ hours.

In a small saucepan over medium heat, combine the soy sauce, brown sugar, rice vinegar and ginger. Bring it to a boil and allow the sauce to cook until it begins to thicken and reduce down, 1 to 2 minutes. Stir often. When the Brussels sprouts are tender, pour the sauce over them and stir to coat.

NEW YEAR'S EVE SOUP PARTY

For years, we have rung in the New Year with friends and a soup party. I usually make five to six different soups along with some homemade bread or rolls. Since they can never decide which one is their favorite, my family and friends always try a little bit of each one. The Clam Chowder (page 46) and the Roasted Red Pepper Soup (page 51) always seem to be the ones to disappear first.

The slow cooker is the perfect way to prepare and serve soup as it keeps it warm and doesn't burn on the bottom. The Fresh Tomato Pesto Soup (page 49) is one of my favorites, and pairing it with a grilled cheese sandwich is pure comfort food. The Italian Beef and Barley (page 52), Pork Verde Stew (page 58) and Simply Chili (page 57) are heartier soups and are sure to satisfy those family members who may think soup isn't a meal!

CLAM CHOWDER

At our annual soup party, this soup is always the first one to disappear. The addition of pepper bacon is the secret ingredient in this chowder and really makes a difference. Some of us like our clam chowder thick, and some prefer it a bit thinner. Here, you can easily control the thickness of your chowder by the amount of flour or thickener you use. The soup will tend to thicken as it cools, but if it gets too thick, thin it with some additional clam juice or milk.

SERVES 6 TO 8

1 cup (151 g) chopped onion

1 cup (100 g) chopped celery

½ cup (115 g) butter

1 (24-oz [735-g]) can chopped clams, drained, reserve liquid

3 potatoes, peeled and cubed

½ lb (227 g) pepper bacon, cooked crisp and diced

3 cups (710 ml) whole milk

½ cup (118 ml) half-and-half

¼ cup (31 g) flour

Salt and pepper to taste

In a pan, sauté the onion and celery in butter over medium heat until soft, 3 to 4 minutes.

Drain the clams and reserve the liquid. Add enough water to the liquid to create a total of 3 cups (710 ml). Add the liquid to a 6-quart (6-L) slow cooker along with the clams, potatoes, bacon, milk, half-and-half and the onion and celery mixture.

Cook on high for 3 hours.

Remove 1 cup (240 ml) soup (mostly liquid) and whisk in the flour. Cook for an additional 30 minutes on high to allow the soup to thicken. Add salt and pepper to taste.

FRESH TOMATO PESTO SOUP

This soup is the perfect thing to make when your garden is overflowing with tomatoes. Don't limit yourself to just tomato season for this soup, though! You can make it with canned tomatoes if fresh tomatoes aren't available. When I use fresh tomatoes, I leave the skins on and then use my high-speed blender or immersion blender to purée them after they cook. It leaves a little bit of texture in the soup, which we enjoy, but if you'd prefer a smoother texture to your soup, go ahead and peel the tomatoes. If you don't have a high-speed blender or an immersion blender, you will want to peel the tomatoes. Tomato soup is real comfort food at our house; add a grilled cheese sandwich and I'm a happy camper.

SERVES 6 TO 8

3 lb (1.5 kg) fresh tomatoes, unpeeled and cut into quarters, or 4 cups (643 g) canned whole tomatoes

1 (15-oz [425-g]) can tomato sauce

2 tbsp (32 g) pesto

1 cup (151 g) chopped onion

½ cup (118 ml) chicken broth

4 tsp (13 g) fresh minced garlic

1 tsp salt

1 tbsp (12 g) sugar

1 cup (237 ml) half-and-half

Fresh basil, pine nuts and Parmesan cheese, for garnish

Combine all ingredients except for the half-and-half and garnish into a 6-quart (6-L) slow cooker.

Cook on high for 4 hours.

Transfer the soup to a high-speed blender and purée until smooth. Return it to the slow cooker.

Add the half-and-half and stir. Cook on low for about 30 minutes to bring the soup back up to temperature.

Serve with fresh basil, pine nuts and Parmesan cheese.

CURRIED BUTTERNUT SQUASH SOUP

The combination of curry, cinnamon, cumin, ginger and a dash of red pepper flakes makes for a flavorful and satisfying soup. Peeling the squash is the hardest part of this recipe, and I've got a tip for you to make that job easier. Slice the top and bottom off of the squash and then poke the squash all over with a fork. Place the squash in the microwave and cook on high for about 3 minutes. Let it cool slightly and then use a potato peeler to peel. You'll be amazed by how much easier it is to peel.

SERVES 8

8 cups (1.5 kg) peeled butternut squash, cubed into 1-inch (25-mm) pieces

½ cup (76 g) onion, chopped

2 cups (473 ml) chicken or vegetable broth

2 tsp (5 g) curry powder

⅛ tsp cinnamon

1 tsp salt

½ tsp cumin

¼ tsp fresh minced ginger

2 tbsp (30 ml) honey

¼ to ½ tsp red pepper flakes

1 (13.5-oz [398-ml]) can coconut milk

Sour cream, cilantro and pistachios, for garnish

Place all the ingredients except for the coconut milk and garnishes into a 6-quart (6-L) slow cooker.

Cook on high for 4 hours or until the squash is tender.

Pour half the soup into a high-speed blender or food processer and blend until desired smoothness.

Pour the soup into a bowl and repeat the process with the remaining soup.

Return all of the soup to the slow cooker and stir in the coconut milk.

Cover and cook for an additional 20 to 30 minutes to heat through.

Garnish with sour cream, cilantro and pistachios.

ROASTED RED PEPPER SOUP

If you are a tomato soup fan, you are going to love this Roasted Red Pepper Soup. Roasting the peppers first sweetens them and then deepens the flavor. Topping the soup with sour cream, fresh basil and a little cheese is my favorite way to serve it.

SERVES 6

5 red peppers, quartered and seeded (do not remove the skin)

1 large sweet onion, quartered

6 Roma tomatoes, cut in half

2 tbsp (30 ml) olive oil

1 tsp salt

½ tsp pepper

2 tsp (6 g) fresh minced garlic

6 oz (170 g) tomato paste

2 cups (473 ml) chicken broth

Salt to taste

Sour cream, Parmesan cheese and fresh basil, for garnish

Preheat the oven to 350°F (177°C).

Place the peppers, onion and tomatoes on a baking sheet and toss with olive oil, salt and pepper. Roast the vegetables in the oven for 30 to 40 minutes or until tender and slightly charred.

Place the vegetables into a 6-quart (6-L) slow cooker. Add the garlic, tomato paste and chicken broth.

Cook on low for 6 hours or on high for 3 hours.

Use an immersion blender or high-speed blender to puree the ingredients until smooth and at the desired consistency. Add additional chicken broth to thin the soup if desired. Add additional salt if needed.

Top with sour cream, Parmesan cheese and fresh basil.

ITALIAN BEEF AND BARLEY SOUP

If you know people who don't consider soup a meal, this soup might just change their minds. Thanks to pearl barley and beef, this soup is hearty and rich and the perfect comfort food for a cold winter's night.

SERVES 8

½ cup (62 g) flour

1 tsp garlic powder

1 tsp paprika

2 lb (1 kg) stew meat

3 tbsp (45 ml) olive oil

2 carrots, peeled and sliced

1 cup (151 g) chopped onion

2 (14-oz [397-g]) cans petite dice tomatoes

1 (6-oz [170-g]) can tomato paste

6 cups (1.5 L) beef broth

3 tsp (10 g) fresh minced garlic

2 tsp (5 g) Italian seasoning

2 bay leaves

1 (15-oz [425-g]) can corn, drained

1 cup (184 g) pearl barley, uncooked

Combine the flour with the garlic powder and paprika in a plastic bag. Add the meat and toss to coat.

Heat the olive oil over medium heat in a large pan and cook the meat in a single layer until browned, about 4 to 5 minutes. Repeat as necessary.

Place the meat into a 6-quart (6-L) slow cooker and cover with the carrots and onions.

Mix together the tomatoes, tomato paste, beef broth, garlic, Italian seasoning and bay leaves. Pour the mixture into the slow cooker.

Cook on high for 4 to 5 hours or on low for 7 hours.

Add the corn and barley, and cook for 1 hour on high. If the soup thickens too much after adding the barley, add additional beef broth.

Remove bay leaves before serving.

CORN CHOWDER

This chowder is a hearty and creamy blend of sweet corn, potatoes, oregano and marjoram. The recipe calls for frozen corn, but during corn season, try using fresh sweet corn instead. I love to garnish this chowder with some crispy bacon and green onions for even more flavor. Leftover Maple and Brown Sugar Ham (page 96) would be a nice addition too.

SERVES 10

5 red potatoes, cubed (don't peel)

1 cup (151 g) chopped onion

1 cup (100 g) chopped celery

1 cup (128 g) carrots, peeled and diced

1 lb (454 g) frozen corn

1 (15-oz [425-g]) can creamed corn

1 tsp dried oregano

1 tsp garlic powder

½ tsp dried marjoram

Dash of red pepper flakes

Salt and pepper to taste

3 cups (710 ml) chicken broth

2 tbsp (29 g) butter

2 tbsp (16 g) flour

1 cup (237 ml) half-and-half

Green onions and crisp bacon, for garnish

In a 6-quart (6-L) slow cooker, place the potatoes, onion, celery, carrots and corn. Add seasonings to the chicken broth and pour it over the top of the ingredients in the slow cooker. Place the butter on top.

Cover and cook on low for 7 hours.

Add the flour to the half-and-half and whisk to combine. Pour this into the slow cooker and cook on high for 30 minutes to allow the chowder to thicken. It will thicken more as it cools. If it thickens too much, add some additional chicken broth.

Top with green onions and crisp bacon.

CHICKEN AND WILD RICE SOUP

For years, I worked for a company that has its headquarters in Minnesota, so I visited several times a year. Every time I was there, I had to have at least one bowl of chicken and wild rice soup, which is basically the Minnesota state soup. When I stopped working for that company, I had to start making it at home and using the slow cooker is the perfect way to cook wild rice soup.

SERVES 8 TO 10

3 skinless, boneless chicken breasts

6 cups (1.5 L) chicken broth

½ cup (76 g) chopped onion

1 cup (100 g) chopped celery

1 cup (128 g) chopped carrots

2 tsp (20 g) fresh minced garlic

1 tsp herbes de Provence

½ tsp dried thyme leaves

½ tsp dried mustard

½ tsp salt

¼ to ½ tsp pepper

¾ cup (120 g) wild rice

3 tbsp (43 g) butter

¼ cup (31 g) all-purpose flour

1 cup (236 ml) half-and-half

1 cup (170 g) slivered almonds, for garnish

Fresh parsley, for garnish

Add all the ingredients except for the butter, half-and-half and flour into a 6-quart (6-L) slow cooker. Cook on low for 4 hours.

Remove the chicken and shred it. Return the chicken to the slow cooker.

In a small pan, melt the butter over medium heat and stir in the flour. Mix for 1 minute.

Whisk in the half-and-half and stir until slightly thickened (it will thicken more once it's added to the slow cooker).

Add the mixture to the soup, stir and allow it to thicken for 30 minutes.

Serve with slivered almonds and fresh parsley on top.

SIMPLY CHILI

Nothing beats a simple, delicious chili for a cold winter night or some football-watching fun! We prefer kidney beans, but you can use your favorite bean or a combination of two different kinds. The chipotle chili powder gives it a bit of a smoky flavor, and the cilantro adds a nice brightness.

SERVES 6 TO 8

2 lb (1 kg) lean ground beef

1 cup (151 g) chopped onion

4 tsp (13 g) fresh minced garlic

2 (14.5-oz [411-g]) cans diced tomatoes

1 (6-oz [170-g]) can tomato paste

2 (15.25-oz [425-g]) cans kidney beans

1 cup (175 g) chopped green pepper

1 (12-oz [340-g]) can tomato sauce

1 tbsp (7 g) cocoa powder

¼ tsp chipotle chili powder

2 tbsp (27 g) brown sugar

1 tsp dried Mexican oregano

1 tsp salt

½ tsp black pepper

2 tsp (5 g) cumin

¼ cup (59 ml) red wine vinegar

¼ cup (109 g) chili powder

1 cup (50 g) cilantro chopped, plus more for garnish

Brown the ground beef, onion and garlic in a large pan over medium heat. Drain.

Place the meat, onions and garlic into a 6-quart (6-L) slow cooker. Add the diced tomatoes, tomato paste, kidney beans, green pepper, tomato sauce, cocoa powder, chipotle chili powder, brown sugar, oregano, salt, pepper, cumin, vinegar, chili powder and cilantro.

Cook on low for 8 hours or on high for 4 to 5 hours.

To thicken, remove the lid for the last 30 to 60 minutes.

Top with additional cilantro for garnish.

PORK VERDE STEW

This stew is a blend of all my favorite Mexican flavors—cumin, Mexican oregano, green chilies, jalapeños and tomatillos. Chunks of pork, potato and tomato make this more of a stew than a soup. Sometimes I like to serve this stew over rice to give it some additional texture.

SERVES 8

1 tbsp (15 ml) canola oil

Salt and pepper to taste

1½ lb (680 g) pork shoulder roast, cut into 1-inch (25-mm) cubes

5 tomatillos, husked, cut in half and blended

4 Yukon gold potatoes, cut into 1-inch (25-mm) cubes

3 cups (710 ml) chicken broth

½ cup (76 g) diced onion

2 tsp (6 g) fresh minced garlic

2 tsp (5 g) Mexican oregano

1 tsp cumin

½ tsp salt

¼ tsp pepper

4 oz (127 g) diced green chilies

1 jalapeño, seeded and diced

Sour cream and fresh minced cilantro, for garnish

Heat the oil in a large frying pan over medium heat. Salt and pepper the pork and add it to the hot oil. Cook the meat until lightly browned on both sides, about 2 to 3 minutes per side.

Place the meat into a 6-quart (6-L) slow cooker.

Mix together the remaining ingredients except for the sour cream and cilantro and add it to the slow cooker. Stir to mix.

Cook on low for 6 to 7 hours or on high for 3 to 4 hours.

Serve with a spoonful of sour cream and cilantro.

CHICKEN PARMESAN SOUP

Enjoy all the amazing flavors of chicken Parmesan in soup form. Everything is cooked right in the slow cooker, including the chicken and pasta. I love to add plenty of cheese to each bowl and place it under the broiler to let the cheese get all hot and bubbly.

SERVES 8 TO 10

2 boneless, skinless chicken breasts, about 1½ lb (680 g)

4 cups (946 ml) chicken broth

3 tsp (10 g) minced garlic

2 (14.5-oz [411-g]) cans petite dice tomatoes

1 (6-oz [170-g]) can tomato paste

½ cup (76 g) chopped onion

½ tsp dried fennel

1 tsp dried marjoram

1 tsp dried oregano

1 tsp dried basil

2 tsp (5 g) dried parsley

4 oz (120 g) rotini pasta

½ cup (90 g) grated Parmesan cheese, divided

1 cup (130 g) grated mozzarella cheese, divided

Fresh basil, chopped, for garnish

Place the chicken in the bottom of a 6-quart (6-L) slow cooker and cover with the chicken broth, garlic, tomatoes, tomato paste, onions and seasonings.

Cook on low for 3 to 4 hours.

Remove the chicken, shred it with two forks, and then return it to the slow cooker. Add the pasta and ⅓ cup (60 g) Parmesan cheese, and cook on high for 30 minutes or until the pasta is cooked al dente. If the soup becomes too thick, thin it with some additional chicken broth.

Serve topped with the remaining Parmesan cheese and the mozzarella cheese. Allow the cheese to melt on top of the soup slightly, or place it under the broiler to melt it and get it bubbly.

Top with fresh basil.

*See photo on page 2.

VALENTINE'S DINNER

Whether you are celebrating as a family or as a romantic dinner for two at home, you will find plenty of delicious menu options in this section. Pasta speaks my love language and the Bolognese Sauce (page 64), Lemon-Garlic Chicken Pasta (page 70) or the Creamy Beef Stroganoff (page 62) is a perfect way to celebrate for me. The sure way to my husband's heart is with Smothered Pork Chops (page 65) served with some Herb Roasted Potatoes (page 68) and Honey Dijon Brussels Sprouts (page 68).

Of course you can't celebrate Valentine's Day without chocolate and the Chocolate-Peanut Butter Pudding Cake (page 74) is sure to melt anyone's heart! If you are not a chocolate lover, be sure and try the Dulce de Leche and Caramelized Apples (page 69).

CREAMY BEEF STROGANOFF

Beef stroganoff is the ultimate comfort food. This simple and rich version has tender pieces of meat and mushrooms with a creamy sauce that is perfect served over noodles.

SERVES 4

⅓ cup (42 g) flour

½ tsp paprika

½ tsp garlic powder

2 lb (1 kg) stew meat

2 tbsp (30 ml) olive oil

½ cup (76 g) chopped onion

1¼ cups (296 ml) beef broth

2 tsp (10 g) salt

1 tsp pepper

1 tsp onion powder

1 tsp dried parsley flakes

½ tsp dried thyme leaves

½ tsp paprika

2 tbsp (30 ml) Worcestershire sauce

8 oz (227 g) mushrooms, cut in half

½ cup (60 g) sour cream

Fresh parsley, for garnish

Place the flour, paprika and garlic powder in a large plastic bag. Add the stew meat and toss to coat.

Heat the olive oil over medium heat in a large frying pan and add the meat. Cook until lightly browned, 3 to 4 minutes.

Add the meat and onions to a 6-quart (6-L) slow cooker.

Mix together the broth, salt, pepper, onion powder, parsley, thyme, paprika and Worcestershire sauce. Pour it over the meat mixture and stir to combine.

Cook on low for 5 to 6 hours. During the last hour of cooking, add the mushrooms.

Add the sour cream at the end and stir to mix.

Serve over noodles and garnish with fresh parsley.

BOLOGNESE SAUCE

This chunky pasta sauce uses a combination of hamburger and pork sausage for even more flavor. Cooking it low and slow in the slow cooker gives this sauce a rich, deep flavor. Serve it over your favorite pasta.

SERVES 8

1 lb (454 g) lean hamburger

1 lb (454 g) Italian pork sausage

1 cup (151 g) chopped onion

3 tsp (10 g) fresh minced garlic

1 (28-oz [784-g]) can crushed tomatoes

1 (28-oz [784-g]) can diced tomatoes

1 cup (237 ml) water

1 (15-oz [425-g]) can tomato sauce

2 bay leaves

1 tsp dried fennel seed

1 tbsp (2 g) dried parsley

1½ tsp (1 g) dried oregano

1½ tsp (1 g) dried basil

4 tbsp (48 g) sugar

Salt and pepper to taste

1 (6-oz [170-g]) can tomato paste for thickening (if needed)

Parmesan cheese, grated, for garnish

Brown the hamburger and sausage with the onion and garlic in a medium-size pan over medium heat, 3 to 4 minutes. Place the meat mixture into the slow cooker.

Add the crushed tomatoes, diced tomatoes, water, tomato sauce, bay leaves, fennel seed, parsley, oregano, basil, sugar, salt and pepper, and stir to combine.

Place a double layer of paper towels over the slow cooker but under the lid (don't allow it to touch the sauce). This will help absorb the water that collects in the lid and prevent it from falling into the sauce. If you can, replace the paper towels halfway through the cooking process.

Cook on low for 6 hours. For the last hour, remove the lid and allow the sauce to thicken up a bit, if desired. If you would like it thicker, add the can of tomato paste, stir to incorporate and allow it to cook for 30 minutes.

Remove the bay leaves, serve over pasta and garnish with Parmesan cheese.

SMOTHERED PORK CHOPS

Smothered Pork Chops are the perfect comfort food, especially when they are served over potatoes. Smothered in onions, veggies and gravy, these pork chops go perfectly with mashed potatoes, which provide a vehicle for all that lovely gravy you will end up with.

SERVES 4

4 tbsp (60 ml) olive oil, divided

2 yellow onions, sliced

4 tsp (10 g) granulated sugar

3 tsp (10 g) fresh minced garlic

1½ tsp salt, divided

1 tsp dried rosemary

1 tsp smoked paprika

1 tsp garlic powder

½ tsp pepper

4 tbsp (31 g) flour

4 to 5 bone-in blade-cut pork chops

3 cups (709 ml) chicken broth

2 tbsp (30 ml) Worcestershire sauce

1 cup (128 g) chopped carrots

1 cup (175 g) chopped red pepper

Fresh parsley, for garnish

In a frying pan, add 2 tablespoons (30 ml) of olive oil over medium heat, cook the onions and sugar until the onions begin to soften, 3 to 4 minutes. Add the garlic, ½ teaspoon of salt and rosemary. Cook for a few more minutes and then place it in the slow cooker.

Put the remaining salt, smoked paprika, garlic powder, pepper and flour into a large zippered plastic bag. Add the pork chops and shake to coat the pork chops.

Add the remaining 2 tablespoons (30 ml) of olive oil to the frying pan and add the pork chops. Brown the chops on all sides over medium heat, 2 to 3 minutes each side.

Add the chicken broth, Worcestershire sauce, carrots and red pepper to a 6-quart (6-L) slow cooker. Stir to combine and add the pork chops.

Cook on high for 4 hours. To thicken the gravy, remove the pork chops from the slow cooker and pour the remaining gravy into a pan.

Add any remaining seasoned flour that you used to coat the pork chops, about 2 tablespoons (15 g) or so. If you don't have that much left, just add 2 tablespoons (15 g) of flour to the liquid. Stir over medium heat to thicken the gravy, 2 to 3 minutes.

This is best served over mashed potatoes. Garnish with fresh parsley.

CASHEW NUT RICE PILAF

We are big rice eaters in our house, and this recipe is a variation of a recipe that was given to my mom years ago by a Lebanese friend. It is our go-to rice and the one my children request over and over. The addition of vermicelli, or thin spaghetti, adds a fun texture.

SERVES 10 TO 12

½ cup (45 g) vermicelli noodles, broken in pieces

¼ cup (57 g) butter

2 cups (421 g) long grain rice

1 tsp seasoning salt

1 tsp minced onion

4 cups (949 ml) chicken broth

Half a lemon, zested

½ cup (56 g) cashews

4 green onions, chopped

In a saucepan, brown the vermicelli in butter over medium heat until golden brown, 3 to 4 minutes. Stir constantly to prevent burning.

Place the rice, browned vermicelli, salt, minced onion, chicken broth and lemon zest in a 6-quart (6-L) slow cooker. I like to use a slow cooker liner to prevent the rice from sticking to the slow cooker. If you are not using a liner, be sure to spray the slow cooker with cooking spray.

Cook on high for 1 to 2 hours.

Stir in the cashews and green onions and serve.

HONEY DIJON BRUSSELS SPROUTS

Honey and mustard is a favorite flavor combination that works perfectly with Brussels sprouts. You've got some sweet, some tangy and some savory. All your taste buds are covered!

SERVES 6

1½ lb (680 g) Brussels sprouts

2 tbsp (30 ml) olive oil

½ tsp salt

¼ tsp black pepper

2 tbsp (30 ml) honey

2 tbsp (30 ml) Dijon mustard

¼ tsp smoked paprika

¼ tsp garlic powder

¼ tsp onion powder

Cut off the ends of the Brussels sprouts and then cut them in half lengthwise. Place the sprouts in a 6-quart (6-L) slow cooker and toss with the olive oil, salt and pepper.

Mix together the honey, mustard, smoked paprika, garlic powder and onion powder, and pour it over the sprouts.

Cook on high for 1½ hours or on low for 3 hours. Stir occasionally to coat the sprouts.

HERB ROASTED POTATOES

I love the combination of thyme, oregano and marjoram, but you can use your favorite herb combination. These potatoes are our go-to potato dish and they go with everything. If you end up with some extra moisture in the slow cooker, remove the lid for the last 30 minutes of cooking.

SERVES 8

16 small red potatoes, about 3 lb (1.5 kg)

2 tbsp (30 ml) olive oil

1 tsp dried thyme

1 tsp dried oregano

1 tsp dried marjoram

2 tsp (6 g) fresh minced garlic

Salt and pepper to taste

Quarter the potatoes and place them in a 6-quart (6-L) slow cooker. Drizzle the olive oil over the potatoes and stir to coat. Sprinkle the potatoes with the dried herbs and garlic, and stir to coat.

Cook on low for 4 to 5 hours or on high for 3 hours or until the potatoes are nice and tender but not mushy. Add salt and pepper as needed.

DULCE DE LECHE AND CARAMELIZED APPLES

I was first introduced to dulce de leche during a trip to Argentina, where they ate it on everything. At breakfast, there would be a big bowl of dulce de leche on the buffet table so you could spread it on your toast or drizzle it over fruit. At dinner, dessert usually included dulce de leche in some form. The secret to making your own dulce de leche is to cook it low and slow, so the slow cooker is the perfect place. My favorite way to enjoy dulce de leche is with caramelized apples over vanilla ice cream.

SERVES 4 TO 6

DULCE DE LECHE

2 (14-oz [396-g]) cans sweetened condensed milk

Water

CARAMELIZED APPLES

2 tbsp (29 g) butter

4 Granny Smith apples, peeled, cored and cut into ¼-inch (6-mm) slices

2 tsp (8 g) sugar

Vanilla ice cream

For the dulce de leche, remove the labels from the cans of sweetened condensed milk and place the unopened cans in a 6-quart (6-L) slow cooker. Lay them on their sides.

Cover the cans with water. The water level should be 1 inch (25 mm) above the cans. Check a few times during the cooking process to make sure the water level does not go down.

Cook on low for 10 hours. Remove the cans from the water and allow them to cool.

Open the cans and grab a spoon!

For the caramelized apples, melt the butter in a frying pan over medium heat and add the apples. Sauté for about 10 minutes or until the apple slices are softened and lightly browned.

Sprinkle the sugar over the apples and cook for 3 to 4 minutes until the sugar begins to caramelize and the apples are nicely browned and softened but not mushy.

Spoon the apples over ice cream and drizzle with the dulce de leche.

LEMON–GARLIC CHICKEN PASTA

Thanks to the lemon juice, zest and lemon pepper, this lemon-garlic chicken packs a lemony punch! You can use breast or thigh meat, although I prefer thigh meat. Serve over pasta and the leftover juice in the slow cooker becomes your pasta sauce.

SERVES 4 TO 6

2 lb (1 kg) boneless, skinless chicken breasts or thighs

1 tsp lemon pepper

1 tsp dried oregano

½ tsp salt

2 tbsp (29 g) butter

1½ cups (354 ml) chicken broth

¼ cup (59 ml) fresh lemon juice

1 tsp lemon zest

2 tsp (6 g) fresh minced garlic

2 tbsp (19 g) cornstarch

Fresh parsley, for garnish

Sprinkle the chicken with the lemon pepper, oregano and salt on both sides.

Melt the butter over medium heat in a large frying pan and brown the chicken on both sides, about 3 to 5 minutes per side.

Place the chicken in a 6-quart (6-L) slow cooker.

Add the chicken broth, lemon juice, zest and garlic to the pan the chicken was in. Bring it to a boil and scrape up all the goodness on the bottom of the pan. Pour the sauce over the chicken in the slow cooker.

Cover and cook on low for 3 to 4 hours (breasts will take more like 4 hours). The chicken will be tender and pull apart easily.

Remove the chicken and ½ cup (118 ml) of juice from the slow cooker. Add the cornstarch to the juice and then return it to the slow cooker. Cook the sauce for 30 minutes on high to allow it to thicken.

Pull the chicken apart and put it back into the sauce. Pour it over the pasta and mix to combine. Garnish with fresh parsley.

CHICKEN TIKKA MASALA

My college kids are the ones who introduced me to Indian food, and it quickly became one of our favorites. Tikka masala seems to be everyone's favorite Indian dish in our family. I prefer to use chicken thighs in this dish because they don't dry out as quickly as chicken breasts. This dish has a little heat, but you can reduce the paprika for less heat, if desired. I love to serve it with basmati rice and some soft wrap bread.

SERVES 4 TO 6

8 boneless, skinless chicken thighs

2 (15-oz [425-g]) cans diced tomatoes

1 cup (151 g) diced onion

2 tbsp (15 g) garam masala

3 tsp (10 g) fresh minced garlic

1 tsp fresh minced ginger

1½ tsp (8 g) salt

2 tbsp (27 g) brown sugar

1 tsp paprika

1 tsp cumin

2 tbsp (33 g) tomato paste

½ cup (60 g) plain Greek yogurt

½ cup (25 g) cilantro, chopped

Trim the fat from the chicken thighs and cut into 1-inch (25-mm) pieces. Thigh meat is easier to cut if it is partially frozen.

Place the chicken in a 6-quart (6-L) slow cooker. Add all the tomatoes, onion, garam masala, garlic, ginger, salt, brown sugar, paprika, cumin, tomato paste and yogurt, and stir to mix.

Cook on low for 4 to 5 hours. Add the cilantro or use it as garnish.

Serve with rice and soft wrap bread.

CHOCOLATE-PEANUT BUTTER PUDDING CAKE

There is no better way to show someone how much you love them than with chocolate and peanut butter! This rich, moist cake forms a layer of deliciously thick sauce at the bottom as it cooks. Of course, it is even better when served with ice cream and the sauce is poured over the top.

SERVES 6

1½ cups (187 g) all-purpose flour

½ cup (110 g) dark brown sugar, packed

1 tsp baking powder

1 tsp baking soda

¼ tsp salt

2 tbsp (14 g) cocoa powder

¾ cup (135 g) creamy peanut butter

½ cup (122 g) Greek yogurt

2 tbsp (29 ml) canola oil

1 tsp vanilla extract

2 tbsp (30 ml) hot water

½ cup (90 g) semisweet chocolate chips or peanut butter chips

¾ cup (144 g) granulated sugar

5 tbsp (35 g) unsweetened cocoa powder

2 cups (473 ml) boiling water

Ice cream, optional

Coat the inside of a 6-quart (6-L) slow cooker with cooking spray.

In a bowl, whisk together the flour, brown sugar, baking powder, baking soda, salt and cocoa powder.

In another bowl, combine the peanut butter, Greek yogurt, oil, vanilla extract and hot water.

Mix together the contents of the two bowls and stir to combine (it will be thick like cookie dough). Fold in the chips.

Spread the batter evenly on the bottom of the slow cooker.

Whisk together the granulated sugar, cocoa powder and boiling water until it's combined, and pour it over the top of the batter in the slow cooker.

Place a cotton or paper towel between the slow cooker and the lid to absorb condensation. Cook on high for 1½ hours. The cake will begin to pull away from the sides of the cooker when it is done.

Spoon the cake into a bowl and top with the sauce that formed on the bottom of the cooker. For an extra treat, top the cake with ice cream before adding the sauce.

CHINESE NEW YEAR

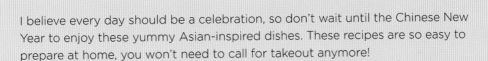

I believe every day should be a celebration, so don't wait until the Chinese New Year to enjoy these yummy Asian-inspired dishes. These recipes are so easy to prepare at home, you won't need to call for takeout anymore!

Our go-to Chinese food order is usually Beef and Broccoli (page 81), which is my husband's favorite, and Cashew Nut Chicken (page 80), which is my favorite. We usually fight over the last few cashews! Our kids always seem to love Sweet and Sour Pork (page 90) and I can't decide if it's the color they love or the pieces of pineapple. If you're looking for a little heat, be sure and try the General Tso's Chicken (page 88).

A pot of rice is the only other thing you need to enjoy a delicious meal of Chinese food, but if you are looking for a lower carb option, be sure and try the Easy Weeknight Chicken Lettuce Wraps (page 87).

GINGER SESAME GLAZED PORK TENDERLOIN

I love the slow cooker for pork tenderloin because it helps keep this tender cut of meat juicy and full of flavor, and it only takes 3 hours on low heat. Use a meat thermometer to check your meat temperature, as pork needs to be between 145° and 165°F (62° and 74°C) to be fully cooked. The ginger sesame glaze adds a lovely Asian flavor to the meat.

SERVES 4 TO 5

2 tbsp (24 g) brown sugar

1 tsp salt

½ tsp dried ginger

1 tsp garlic powder

¼ tsp black pepper

¼ tsp crushed red pepper

1½ to 2 lb (0.5 to 1 kg) pork tenderloin

½ cup (118 ml) water

GINGER SESAME GLAZE

½ cup (72 g) brown sugar

1 tsp sesame oil

1 tsp fresh minced garlic

1 tbsp (8 g) cornstarch

¼ cup (59 ml) white or rice wine vinegar

½ cup (118 ml) chicken broth

2 tbsp (30 ml) soy sauce

½ tsp dried ginger

Toasted sesame seeds, for garnish

Green onion, sliced, for garnish

In a bowl, combine the brown sugar, salt, ginger, garlic, black pepper and crushed red pepper to form a rub.

Place the pork in a 6-quart (6-L) slow cooker and rub the seasoning over all sides of the pork.

Pour in ½ cup (118 ml) of water, but do not pour directly over the pork or you will wash off the rub.

Cook on low for 3 hours.

To make the glaze, combine the brown sugar, sesame oil, garlic, cornstarch, vinegar, broth, soy sauce and ginger in a saucepan. Stir over medium heat until the mixture boils and thickens, about 5 minutes.

Preheat the broiler.

Remove the meat from the slow cooker and place it on a foil-lined baking sheet. Brush the meat with the glaze and place it under the broiler until the glaze bubbles and begins to caramelize, 1 to 2 minutes. Brush the meat two more times, placing it under the broiler each time until the glaze bubbles and begins to caramelize. Watch continually as the sugar from the glaze can burn quickly.

Remove the meat from the broiler, slice it and sprinkle it with toasted sesame seeds and green onions.

CASHEW NUT CHICKEN

This is by far my favorite Chinese food, and the one I always order first when we go out for Chinese. Being able to make this delicious and easy version at home allows me to enjoy my favorite as much as I want. I'm always a little protective of my cashews, so don't try to steal any off my plate! (My husband learned the hard way early in our marriage.) I always add a few extra cashews, so there are plenty to go around.

SERVES 4 TO 6

3 tbsp (28 g) cornstarch

½ tsp pepper

2 lb (1 kg) boneless, skinless chicken thighs cut into 1-inch (25-mm) pieces

1 tbsp (15 ml) canola oil

1 cup (236 ml) tomato sauce

⅓ cup (63 g) sugar

2 tbsp (30 ml) rice wine vinegar

1 tsp garlic powder

½ cup (118 ml) soy sauce

½ tsp fresh minced ginger

1 cup (150 g) cashews

Green onion, for garnish

Mix together the cornstarch and pepper and put it in a large resealable food storage bag. Add the chicken and shake to coat.

Heat the canola oil in a pan over medium heat. Brown the chicken lightly on both sides, 2 to 3 minutes. Place the chicken pieces in a 6-quart (6-L) slow cooker.

Combine the tomato sauce, sugar, vinegar, garlic powder, soy sauce and ginger, and pour the mixture over the chicken. Stir in the cashews or use the cashews as garnish.

Cook on low for 3 to 4 hours. Serve over rice and garnish with green onion and cashews if they weren't already added to the slow cooker.

ASIAN BBQ CHICKEN

This dish is a fun twist on classic BBQ chicken. Add some stir-fried or roasted veggies for a complete meal.

SERVES 8

3 lb (1.5 kg) boneless chicken thighs

Salt and pepper to taste

¾ cup (177 ml) honey

⅓ cup (78 ml) ketchup

½ cup (118 ml) soy sauce

2 tsp (10 ml) rice wine vinegar

1 tbsp (5 g) fresh minced ginger

2 tsp (6 g) fresh minced garlic

1 tsp hot chili garlic sauce

1 tbsp (6 g) lemon zest

2 tbsp (19 g) cornstarch

Trim the excess fat from the chicken thighs. Sprinkle the chicken with salt and pepper and place them in a 6-quart (6-L) slow cooker.

Mix together the remaining ingredients except the cornstarch. Cook on high for 2 to 3 hours or on low for 4 to 5 hours.

Remove the chicken and shred it with a fork.

Add the cornstarch to the remaining liquid in the slow cooker and cook on high for 15 to 30 minutes, or until the sauce thickens.

Serve over rice, on a sandwich or in a salad.

BEEF AND BROCCOLI

This is one of our favorite dishes to get whenever we go out for Chinese or get takeout.

SERVES 4

1½ lb (680 g) flank steak, cut into strips across the grain and then into 2-inch (5-cm) pieces

1 cup (237 ml) chicken broth

½ cup (118 ml) soy sauce

⅓ cup (73 g) packed brown sugar

1 tbsp (15 ml) sesame oil

3 tsp (10 g) fresh minced garlic

1 tsp fresh minced ginger

¼ tsp red chili flakes

3 tbsp (28 g) cornstarch

3 to 4 cups (525 to 700 g) broccoli florets

Place the meat, broth, soy sauce, brown sugar, sesame oil, garlic, ginger and red chili flakes into a 6-quart (6-L) slow cooker and cook on low for 3 hours.

Remove about ⅓ cup (78 ml) liquid from the slow cooker and mix in the cornstarch. Return the mixture to the slow cooker and stir to incorporate. Cook for 30 minutes on high to allow the sauce to thicken up.

While the sauce is thickening, steam the broccoli. I like to put it into a microwave-safe dish with 1 to 2 tablespoons (15 to 30 ml) water, cover the dish with a lid or a wet paper towel and microwave for 4 to 5 minutes or until the broccoli is fork tender.

Mix the broccoli in with the meat in the slow cooker and serve over rice.

ASIAN PEPPER STEAK

You can play around with your pepper combination in this dish depending on your taste preferences, but we prefer using red, yellow or orange peppers. Green peppers work too if they are your favorite, or go crazy and use all of them! The peppers bring some great color and flavor to this dish.

SERVES 4 TO 6

3 lb (1.5 kg) sirloin steak

4 tbsp (40 g) cornstarch, divided

2 tbsp (30 ml) canola oil

2 tsp (6 g) minced garlic

1 cup (151 g) diced onion

1 red bell pepper, sliced

1 yellow bell pepper, sliced

2 tbsp (30 ml) Worcestershire sauce

1 (14.5-oz [411-g]) can stewed tomatoes

2 tbsp (30 ml) oyster sauce

4 tbsp (48 g) brown sugar

½ cup (118 ml) soy sauce

Salt and pepper to taste

Sprinkle both sides of the steak with 2 tablespoons (20 g) cornstarch and pat into the meat.

Heat the oil in a heavy pan and cook the meat over medium heat until lightly brown on both sides, 2 to 3 minutes.

Cut the steaks into 1-inch (25-mm)-wide strips after browning. Place the steak strips into the slow cooker and add the remaining ingredients except the remaining cornstarch.

Cook on low for 6 hours or on high for 4 hours.

In the last hour, remove ¼ cup (60 ml) liquid from the slow cooker and stir in 2 tablespoons (20 g) cornstarch. Return it to the slow cooker and stir. It will thicken up as it continues to cook for the last hour.

SESAME CHICKEN

This recipe has been a favorite at our house for a long time. It uses chicken thighs, which I am a big fan of, but if you prefer chicken breasts, feel free to substitute. When topped with chopped green onions and sesame seeds, it makes for a pretty presentation, too! Serve it over rice.

SERVES 4 TO 6

8 boneless, skinless chicken thighs or 2 chicken breasts, about 2 lb (1 kg) total

Salt and pepper to taste

½ cup (76 g) chopped onion

3 tsp (10 g) fresh minced garlic

1 cup (237 ml) honey or ¾ cup (165 g) brown sugar

¼ cup (60 ml) ketchup

½ cup (118 ml) soy sauce

2 tbsp (30 ml) olive oil

1 tsp sesame oil

1 tsp chili paste

4 tsp (13 g) cornstarch

⅓ cup (78 ml) water

1 tbsp (15 g) sesame seeds

3 green onions, chopped

Place the chicken in a 6-quart (6-L) slow cooker. Season the chicken with salt and pepper.

In a bowl, combine the onion, garlic, honey, ketchup, soy sauce, olive oil, sesame oil and chili paste, and pour it over the chicken.

Cook on low for 3 to 4 hours or on high for 2 hours. Remove the chicken and shred it.

In a small bowl, combine the cornstarch and water.

Pour the sauce from the slow cooker into a saucepan and add the cornstarch mixture. Stir to combine over medium heat. Cook for about 10 minutes or until it has thickened, stirring often. Pour it over the chicken.

Serve over rice and sprinkle with sesame seeds and green onions.

EASY CHICKEN LETTUCE WRAPS

Adding broccoli slaw and slivered almonds near the end of the cooking time gives these lettuce wraps lots of great flavor and texture. This dish will benefit by stirring several times during the cooking process, too. Wrap the meat mixture up in a crisp lettuce leaf or serve over rice.

SERVES 4 TO 6

2 lb (1 kg) ground chicken or turkey

1 cup (151 g) chopped onion

1 red pepper, diced

3 tsp (10 g) fresh minced garlic

1 tsp fresh minced ginger

¼ cup (60 ml) hoisin sauce

2 tsp (10 ml) rice wine vinegar

½ cup (118 ml) soy sauce

1 tbsp (12 g) granulated sugar

1 tbsp (14 g) brown sugar

1 tbsp (15 ml) honey

2 tsp (10 ml) sesame oil

1 (12-oz [340-g]) bag broccoli slaw (use as much or as little as you like)

½ cup (63 g) slivered almonds

2 heads butter or iceberg lettuce

Place the meat, onion and red pepper into a 6-quart (6-L) slow cooker and stir to combine.

Combine the garlic, ginger, hoisin sauce, vinegar, soy sauce, sugars, honey and sesame oil in a bowl. Pour it over the meat mixture and stir to combine.

Cook on low for 4 hours or on high for 2 hours. Stir several times during the cooking time if possible.

After the meat is cooked, add your desired amount of broccoli slaw to the chicken mixture. Cook an additional 30 minutes if desired or serve it crispy.

Garnish with almonds and serve warm inside a lettuce leaf.

GENERAL TSO'S CHICKEN

This sweet and spicy Chinese classic is always popular and works great in a slow cooker. Coating the chicken with cornstarch and frying it in some oil before putting it in the slow cooker gives the meat a better texture and flavor.

SERVES 4

½ cup (76 g) cornstarch

1 tsp salt

1 tsp pepper

1 tsp garlic powder

2 lb (1 kg) boneless, skinless chicken breasts or thighs, cut into 1-inch (25-mm) pieces

2 tbsp (30 ml) canola oil

½ cup (118 ml) hoisin sauce

¼ cup (60 ml) soy sauce

¼ cup (36 g) brown sugar

¼ cup (60 ml) rice vinegar

1 tsp fresh minced garlic

½ tsp fresh minced ginger

½ tsp orange zest

1 tsp sesame oil

Green onions, for garnish

Combine the cornstarch, salt, pepper and garlic powder in a large plastic zippered bag. Add the chicken pieces and shake to coat.

Heat the canola oil in a large frying pan over medium-high heat. Cook the pieces of chicken in the oil until they just begin to brown, 2 to 3 minutes.

Remove the chicken from the pan and place it onto some paper towels to drain. Place the chicken into a 6-quart (6-L) slow cooker.

Mix together the sauces, brown sugar, vinegar, garlic, ginger, zest and sesame oil, and pour it over the chicken. Stir the chicken to coat.

Cook on low for 3 to 4 hours or on high for 2 hours. Stir several times during the cooking time if possible.

Top with chopped green onions and serve over rice.

MONGOLIAN BEEF

Mongolian Beef is always one of our choices when we go out for Chinese takeout. This make-at-home version was so popular at our house, my husband may refuse to ever go out for Chinese takeout again! Add some steamed vegetables to the meat when it is done if you'd like, or I like to garnish with some green onions and sesame seeds.

SERVES 4

1½ lb (680 g) flank steak, cut across the grain into 1-inch (25-mm) pieces

¼ cup (30 g) flour

1 tbsp (15 ml) canola oil

½ cup (76 g) diced onion

2 tsp (6 g) fresh minced garlic

½ cup (118 ml) soy sauce

½ cup (118 ml) beef broth

⅓ cup (63 g) granulated sugar

½ tsp fresh minced ginger

1 tbsp (15 ml) chili garlic sauce

1 tsp sesame oil

1 tbsp (10 g) cornstarch

Green onions and sesame seeds, for garnish

Put the steak and flour into a plastic bag and toss to coat. Heat the oil in a pan over medium heat, add the meat and lightly cook until brown, about 2 to 3 minutes.

Add the meat to a 6-quart (6-L) slow cooker.

Mix together the remaining ingredients except the cornstarch and garnishes, and pour it over the meat.

Cook on low for 3 to 4 hours or until the meat is tender.

Remove the meat from the slow cooker and strain the remaining juice. Place 1 cup (237 ml) strained juice into a saucepan and whisk in the cornstarch.

Bring the sauce to a boil over medium heat and stir until the sauce thickens, 1 to 2 minutes. Pour the sauce over the meat.

Top with sliced green onions and sprinkle with sesame seeds. Serve over rice.

SWEET AND SOUR PORK

Sweet and Sour Pork was always one of my kids' favorite dishes whenever we went out for Chinese food. The sweet tangy flavor comes from the pineapple juice and vinegar, and I think the kids really liked the chunks of pineapple the best! No need for takeout when you can make this delicious dish so easily at home.

SERVES 4 TO 6

2 tbsp (16 g) flour

½ tsp salt

¼ tsp pepper

1½ lb (680 g) boneless pork sirloin roast, cut into 1-inch (25-mm) chunks

2 tbsp (30 ml) olive oil

1 red pepper, diced

1 green pepper, diced

1 cup (76 g) diced onion

½ cup (110 g) packed brown sugar

1 (6-oz [170-g]) can tomato paste

1 tsp fresh minced ginger

2 tbsp (30 ml) white wine vinegar

½ cup (118 ml) pineapple juice

½ tsp garlic powder

2 tsp (10 ml) soy sauce

Place the flour, salt and pepper into a large zippered plastic bag. Add the pieces of pork and shake to coat.

Heat the oil in a large pan over medium heat and add the pork. Cook for 1 to 2 minutes per side until the meat is lightly browned.

Place the pork in a 6-quart (6-L) slow cooker. Add the peppers and onion.

Mix together the remaining ingredients, pour it over the pork and stir it to combine.

Cook on low for 4 hours. Serve over rice.

EASTER
BRUNCH/DINNER

At our house, Easter varies between brunch and dinner from year to year, although Easter brunch is my favorite. You will notice a few lemon recipes in this section because lemon and Easter are a perfect combination as far as I'm concerned. Enjoy Lemon Pull-Apart Biscuits (page 94), Rosemary Lemon Roasted Potatoes (page 109) or a Lemon and Blueberry Glazed Coffee Cake (page 101).

Maple and Brown Sugar Ham (page 96) is the traditional main dish of Easter, and you can't forget the Cheesy Scalloped Potatoes (page 99). We often enjoy pork tenderloin for Easter dinner, and Orange-Glazed Pork Tenderloin (page 102) is one of our favorites. Be sure and make up a batch of Ham, Lentil and Vegetable Soup (page 106) with the leftover ham.

Whether you do Easter dinner or brunch, your slow cooker can be a big help with getting the meal on the table.

LEMON PULL-APART BISCUITS

These Lemon Pull-Apart Biscuits may just move to the top of your favorite lemon recipes. Using refrigerated biscuits makes them delicious and easy. The layers of light, fluffy biscuits covered with fragrant lemon sugar and then drizzled with a tart lemon glaze are a dream!

SERVES 4 TO 6

1 (16.3-oz [462-g]) can refrigerated biscuits, jumbo size (8 biscuits)

2 lemons, zested

½ cup (96 g) granulated sugar

¼ cup (57 g) butter, melted

CITRUS GLAZE

1 cup (130 g) powdered sugar

1 tbsp (15 g) butter, melted

2 tbsp (30 ml) fresh lemon juice

Spray a 6-quart (6-L) slow cooker with cooking spray or create a foil slow cooker liner to prevent the biscuits from overcooking on the edges. Use two pieces of foil that are 18 inches (45.5 cm) long. Fold them in half and then fold again so that each foil piece measures 4 × 18 inches (10 × 45.5 cm) long. Place both pieces into the slow cooker so that they line the sides of the slow cooker. Then place a piece of parchment paper in the slow cooker, over the foil.

Cut each biscuit into four pieces. Mix the lemon zest and sugar together.

Place the lemon sugar mixture in a plastic bag, add the biscuit pieces and toss to coat. Place the biscuit pieces in the slow cooker.

Sprinkle the remaining sugar from the bag over the top of the biscuits. Drizzle with the melted butter.

Place a cotton towel or paper towel between the lid and the slow cooker to absorb condensation. Cook on high for 1½ to 2 hours. Remove the lid for the last 15 to 30 minutes of cooking time.

For the glaze, mix together the powdered sugar, butter and lemon juice, and drizzle it over the top of the cooked biscuits.

MAPLE AND BROWN SUGAR HAM

I often make a ham just so I have leftover ham. It is perfect for Ham, Lentil and Vegetable Soup (page 106) as well as cubed up in a quiche or other egg dish. Don't forget a ham and cheese sandwich! You are going to want to drink the yummy juice that forms during cooking, but save some to spoon over the sliced ham when you serve it.

SERVES 8

1 (4- to 5-lb [2- to 2.5-kg]) fully cooked ham

2 cups (473 ml) orange juice

2 cups (440 g) packed brown sugar

1 tbsp (15 ml) spicy brown mustard

4 tsp (20 ml) balsamic vinegar

4 tsp (20 ml) maple syrup

2 tbsp (19 g) cornstarch

3 tbsp (45 ml) water

Remove the ham from its packaging and discard the flavor packet. Place it in a 6-quart (6-L) slow cooker with the cut side down.

Mix together the orange juice, brown sugar, brown mustard, balsamic vinegar and maple syrup. Pour it over the ham.

Cook on low for 4 to 6 hours or until the ham is heated through to 140°F (60°C). If possible, baste the ham with the juice about once an hour.

When the ham reaches the desired temperature, remove it from the slow cooker and cover it with foil to keep it warm. Put the juice into a saucepan.

Add the cornstarch to the water. Mix it to combine and then add it to the juice. Stir it to combine and cook in a small pan over medium heat until it thickens, 2 to 3 minutes.

Pour the sauce over the sliced ham.

BROWNED BUTTER BALSAMIC CARROTS

I love it when I serve a dish and one of my guests asks, "What's that flavor I'm tasting?" when they can't quite put their finger on it. That's what happens with these delicious carrots. The combination of browned butter and balsamic works perfectly yet remains slightly unidentifiable! If you end up with some excess liquid in the bottom of the slow cooker, take the lid off for the last 30 minutes, and it will absorb into the carrots and help glaze them.

SERVES 6

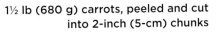

1½ lb (680 g) carrots, peeled and cut into 2-inch (5-cm) chunks

2 tbsp (29 g) butter

¼ tsp salt

¼ tsp pepper

2 tbsp (30 ml) maple syrup

2 tsp (10 ml) balsamic vinegar

Fresh herbs, for garnish

Put the carrots into a 6-quart (6-L) slow cooker.

In a saucepan, add the butter over medium heat and melt. Stir until the butter begins to foam and then turns brown, 1 to 2 minutes. You will end up with some silt in the bottom of the pan, and that's fine—it adds more flavor. You want the butter to be golden yellow. It can go from browned to burned fast, so be sure to watch it.

Add the salt, pepper, maple syrup and vinegar. Stir to combine, pour it over the carrots and stir the carrots to coat.

Cook on high for 3 hours or until tender.

Remove the lid for the last 30 minutes to absorb any excess liquid that may be in the bottom of the slow cooker, and stir several times to coat the carrots during this time.

Sprinkle with fresh herbs of choice before serving, if desired.

CHEESY SCALLOPED POTATOES

Easter dinner would just not be dinner without Cheesy Scalloped Potatoes. These potatoes are the perfect accompaniment to Maple and Brown Sugar Ham (page 96), or you can use up your leftover ham by adding it to this dish.

SERVES 6

3 lb (1.5 kg) red potatoes, sliced evenly, about ⅛ inch (3 mm) thick, divided

½ tsp garlic powder

½ tsp dried oregano

½ tsp salt

¼ tsp pepper

Pinch of red pepper flakes

1 cup (121 g) shredded cheddar/jack cheese mixture, divided

1 cup (236 ml) whipping cream

½ cup (118 ml) half-and-half

¼ cup (45 g) Parmesan cheese

Spray a 6-quart (6-L) slow cooker with cooking spray. Layer half the potato slices in the bottom of the slow cooker.

Combine the garlic powder, oregano, salt, pepper and red pepper flakes in a small container. Sprinkle half of the spice mixture onto the potatoes and top with half of the cheddar/jack cheese mixture. Mix the cream and half-and-half together and pour half the mixture over the potato layer. Repeat with a second layer of potatoes, spices, cheese and cream mixture.

Cook on high for 4 hours. Remove the lid and sprinkle with Parmesan cheese about 15 minutes before the potatoes are done. Replace the lid and allow the cheese to melt.

Remove the lid and let the potatoes rest for about 10 to 15 minutes, allowing the sauce to thicken as the potatoes cool.

GARLIC PARMESAN POTATOES

The combination of smoked paprika and garlic gives these potatoes amazing flavor. Smoked paprika is more intense than regular paprika and will add a nice depth of flavor to your potatoes.

SERVES 4 TO 6

3 lb (1.5 kg) red potatoes, washed and quartered

¼ cup (59 ml) olive oil

½ tsp smoked paprika

1 tsp garlic powder

1 tsp salt

¼ tsp pepper

⅓ cup (59 g) freshly grated Parmesan cheese

Additional cheese for garnish, if desired

Place the potatoes in a 6-quart (6-L) slow cooker and drizzle them with olive oil, seasonings and cheese. Stir to coat evenly.

Cook on high for 3 hours or until the potatoes are tender. Remove the lid for the last 30 minutes of cooking time and allow the moisture to be absorbed. Stir a few times.

Garnish with some additional cheese.

LEMON AND BLUEBERRY GLAZED COFFEE CAKE

We are big lemon fans at our house and for us, spring welcomes in warmer weather and everything lemon. My favorite fruit to pair with lemon is blueberry. This coffee cake would be the perfect addition to your Easter brunch or breakfast any time.

SERVES 6 TO 8

2 eggs

½ cup (60 g) sour cream or plain Greek yogurt

2 tsp (4 g) lemon zest

¼ cup (60 ml) lemon juice or 1 tsp lemon extract

2 tbsp (30 ml) canola oil

1 tsp vanilla

2 cups plus 1 tbsp (258 g) all-purpose flour, divided

1 cup (192 g) granulated sugar

½ tsp salt

1 tsp baking powder

½ tsp baking soda

1 cup (150 g) fresh blueberries

Powdered sugar, for garnish

GLAZE

½ cup (65 g) powdered sugar

Enough lemon juice to make a drizzling consistency

Line a 6-quart (6-L) slow cooker with parchment paper. Mix together the eggs, sour cream, lemon zest, lemon juice, oil and vanilla.

In another bowl, mix together 2 cups (250 g) of flour, sugar, salt, baking powder and baking soda.

Pour the wet mixture into the dry mixture and stir to combine.

Mix together the remaining 1 tablespoon (8 g) of flour with the blueberries to coat them. This will keep the blueberries from sinking to the bottom of the coffee cake.

Gently fold the blueberries into the batter, and then pour the batter into the slow cooker. Put a cotton towel or paper towel over the top of the cooker underneath the lid to absorb moisture.

Cook on high for 2½ hours or until a toothpick comes out clean. Allow it to cool slightly and then dust with powdered sugar.

For the glaze, mix together the powdered sugar and lemon juice, and drizzle it over the coffee cake.

ORANGE-GLAZED PORK TENDERLOIN

This pork tenderloin is amazing! I served it at the rehearsal dinner of a friend's son and it got rave reviews. It's a delicious alternative to ham at Easter. The glaze over the top is so delicious, so don't skip that part! If you are averse to orange, a peach chutney or your favorite marmalade flavor would also be delicious.

SERVES 8 TO 10

2½ lb (1 kg) pork tenderloin

Salt and pepper to taste

1 (18-oz [510-g]) jar orange marmalade, divided

¼ cup (36 g) brown sugar

1 tsp minced garlic

½ tsp salt

¼ cup (59 ml) balsamic vinegar

½ tsp fresh minced ginger

1 cup (237 ml) chicken broth

GLAZE

1 cup (237 ml) juices from the slow cooker

2 tbsp (19 g) cornstarch

½ cup (165 g) orange marmalade

¼ tsp salt

Place the pork tenderloin into a 6-quart (6-L) slow cooker and season with salt and pepper.

Mix together ¾ cup (245 g) of marmalade, sugar, garlic, salt, balsamic vinegar, ginger and broth. Pour the mixture over the pork in the slow cooker.

Cook on low for 3 to 4 hours. I like to be able to slice my pork rather than shred it, so I cook it closer to 3 hours. The pork should be at least 165°F (74°C) when done. Check the meat temperature with a thermometer.

When the pork is finished, pour the remaining liquid from the slow cooker through a strainer.

Brush the meat with the remaining ¼ cup (80 g) of orange marmalade.

For the glaze, put 1 cup (237 ml) of juice into a saucepan and whisk in the cornstarch, ½ cup (165 g) orange marmalade and salt. Bring to a boil and stir until thickened, 2 to 3 minutes. Serve over the pork.

CINNAMON AND WALNUT COFFEE CAKE

Who doesn't love the smell of fresh cinnamon coffee cake baking first thing in the morning? It's the perfect smell to wake up to. This coffee cake is yummy, and it works as breakfast or as a cake for dessert. You choose!

SERVES 6

½ cup (115 g) butter, softened

1 cup (144 g) brown sugar

2 eggs

1 cup (245 g) plain Greek yogurt

1½ tsp (7 ml) vanilla

2 cups (250 g) all-purpose flour

1 tsp baking powder

½ tsp baking soda

½ tsp salt

1 tsp cinnamon

CRUMB TOPPING

¼ cup (25 g) flour

¼ cup (20 g) old-fashioned oats

½ tsp cinnamon

½ cup brown sugar

2 tbsp (29 g) butter

½ cup (58 g) walnuts, chopped

In a bowl, mix together the butter and brown sugar. Add the eggs, beating well. Add the Greek yogurt, vanilla, flour, baking powder, baking soda, salt and cinnamon, and mix well.

For the crumb topping, combine the flour, oats, cinnamon and brown sugar in a bowl. Stir to mix. Add the butter and use a pastry cutter to combine and form coarse crumbs. Add the walnuts.

Create a foil liner for a 6-quart (6-L) slow cooker. Use two pieces of foil that are 18 inches (45.5 cm) long. Fold them in half and then fold again so that each foil piece measures 4 × 18 inches (10 × 45.5 cm) long. Place both pieces into the slow cooker so they line the sides of the slow cooker. Then place a piece of parchment paper inside the slow cooker over the foil and spray with cooking spray.

Pour the coffee cake batter into the slow cooker, spreading it evenly, and sprinkle it with the crumb mixture.

Place a cotton towel or paper towel over the top of the slow cooker and then put on the lid.

Cook on high for 1½ to 2 hours. The cake may seem slightly undercooked in the middle, but it will continue to cook as the cake rests.

Let it sit for 20 to 30 minutes before serving.

HAM, LENTIL AND VEGETABLE SOUP

This soup is the perfect way to use the leftover Maple and Brown Sugar Ham (page 96). In fact, you may cook a ham just so you can make this soup! It's made with chunks of ham, veggies and lentils so you get a hearty and healthy meal all in one.

SERVES 8

2 cups (300 g) ham, cut into cubes

1 cup (200 g) dried lentils

½ cup (76 g) chopped onion

1 cup (100 g) chopped celery

1 cup (128 g) diced carrots

1 (14.5-oz [411-g]) can petite tomatoes

3 tbsp (49 g) tomato paste

1 tsp dried oregano

1 tsp dried thyme leaves

1 tsp dried rosemary

8 cups (2 L) chicken broth

½ tsp black pepper

1 tsp salt

Chopped fresh parsley and grated Parmesan cheese, for garnish

Add all the ingredients except garnishes to a 6-quart (6-L) slow cooker and stir to combine.

Cover and cook on low for 6 to 8 hours or until the lentils and vegetables are tender.

Garnish with the chopped parsley and grated Parmesan cheese.

ROSEMARY LEMON ROASTED POTATOES

Rosemary and lemon are a perfect flavor combination, and you can never have too much lemon at the Easter dinner table as far as I'm concerned. Play around with your herb combos for fun. Maybe try some oregano, marjoram, basil or any other combination of herbs. Removing the lid for the last 30 minutes of cooking gives you a crisper potato and allows the moisture in the cooker to absorb.

SERVES 6

1½ lb (680 g) small Yukon gold potatoes

2 tsp (6 g) fresh minced garlic

1 tbsp (15 ml) olive oil

¼ tsp black pepper

½ tsp salt

1 tsp dried rosemary or 2 tsp (1.5 g) fresh chopped rosemary

1 lemon, sliced

Scrub the potatoes and cut them in half or quarters, depending on the size of your potatoes and the size you desire. They will cook faster the smaller they are, so you may need to adjust cooking time depending on size.

Spray a 6-quart (6-L) slow cooker with cooking spray. Place the potatoes and garlic in the slow cooker and drizzle them with oil while stirring to coat them.

Add pepper, salt and rosemary, and stir.

Place the lemon slices on top, squeeze the juice out of the end pieces onto the potatoes and add them to the slow cooker.

Cook on high for 2½ hours or on low for 4 hours or until the desired tenderness is reached. Stir several times during the cooking time if possible. Remove the lid for the last 30 minutes to allow the moisture to be absorbed.

CINCO DE MAYO

We don't enjoy Mexican food just on Cinco de Mayo at our house; it is definitely a favorite and usually makes an appearance at our dinner table at least a couple of times a week. We like celebrating year round!

One of the most popular recipes at our house, including with my young adult children, is Salsa Verde Carnitas (page 124). Not only is it easy and delicious, but it's so versatile. I serve it over rice, put it in a taco, add it to a burrito or quesadilla or top some nachos with it! You can do the same thing with the Spicy Mexican Beef (page 112), Chili Cilantro Lime Chicken (page 118) or the Pork Tinga with Pineapple (page 114). Make up a big batch and enjoy it for several meals.

Growing up, one of my children's favorite meals was Hawaiian Haystack, a recipe you can find on my blog. I came up with a Mexican version using Mexican Rice (page 117), No-Fry Refried Beans (page 122) and your favorite meat. It's a great way to celebrate Cinco de Mayo, use up leftovers and everyone loves it because they can customize it to their own taste. It's a great dish to feed to a group, too.

SPICY MEXICAN BEEF

You can totally control the heat of this dish with the amount of chili powder and hot pepper sauce you use. We don't like a lot of heat at our house so the heat level on this, as written, is moderate. This is the perfect addition to a taco bar and would make delicious enchiladas, burritos and quesadillas for your Cinco de Mayo celebration.

SERVES 8

1 (4- to 5-lb [2- to 2.5-kg]) chuck roast

Salt and pepper to taste

1 cup (151 g) chopped onion

1 (4.5-oz [127-g]) can green chilies

1 cup (237 ml) beef broth

1 (14.5-oz [411-g]) can diced tomatoes

1 tsp garlic salt

1½ tsp (4 g) cumin

1 tsp Mexican oregano

1 tsp chili powder

¼ cup (60 ml) hot sauce (I prefer Tapatio brand)

Trim the meat of excess fat and season with salt and pepper.

Place the meat in a 6-quart (6-L) slow cooker and cover with onion. In a bowl, mix together the chilies, broth, tomatoes, garlic salt, cumin, Mexican oregano, chili powder and hot sauce, and then pour it over the meat.

Cover and cook on high for 5 hours.

Remove the meat from the cooker and shred it. Return the meat to the slow cooker, stir it into the juices in the cooker and cook on low for 2 hours, allowing the meat to absorb the liquid and additional flavor.

PORK TINGA WITH PINEAPPLE

Pork Tinga with Pineapple is a smoky Mexican-style stew that is tender and delicious, thanks to slow cooking. I love the abundance of flavor in this dish from the chipotle chilies, chorizo and seasonings, along with the sweetness of the pineapple chunks. This is a versatile dish that can be served over rice or added to a tortilla for a burrito or enchilada.

SERVES 6 TO 8

3 lb (1.5 kg) pork butt, picnic roast or shoulder

1½ cups (227 g) chopped onion, divided

4 tsp (12 g) fresh minced garlic, divided

1 tsp dried marjoram

½ tsp dried thyme leaves

2 bay leaves

1 lb (452 g) ground chorizo

1 (28-oz [794-g]) can diced tomatoes with juice

2 chipotle chilies in adobo, seeded and chopped

20 oz (567 g) pineapple chunks

1 tsp Mexican oregano

½ tsp dried marjoram

½ tsp dried thyme

Salt and pepper to taste

Cilantro, for garnish

Add the pork to a 6-quart (6-L) slow cooker. Add 1 cup (151 g) of onion, 2 teaspoons (6 g) of garlic, marjoram, thyme and bay leaves. Add enough water to cover the top of the pork.

Cover and cook on low for 6 to 7 hours or until the pork is tender and pulls apart easily with a fork.

Strain the remaining liquid and set it aside. Remove the pork from the slow cooker and shred it with two forks.

In a pan, over medium heat, cook the chorizo until cooked through, about 5 minutes. Add ½ cup (76 g) of onion and 2 teaspoons (6 g) of garlic to the chorizo and cook for 2 to 3 minutes.

Add the pork back to the slow cooker. Add 2 cups (473 ml) strained pork broth and the cooked chorizo, tomatoes, chipotle chilies, pineapple and remaining seasonings to the slow cooker.

Cook on low for 1 hour. Salt and pepper to taste. Serve with tortillas or over rice. Garnish with cilantro if desired.

LAYERED BEEF ENCHILADAS

Enchiladas are my favorite Mexican dish. I love how easy it is to make enchiladas in the slow cooker by just layering them instead of rolling them. Spicy Mexican Beef (page 112) is the perfect filling for layered enchiladas. You can use canned black beans, or if you have leftover Cilantro Black Beans (page 122), use them!

SERVES 6 TO 8

3 cups (747 g) Spicy Mexican Beef (page 112)

1 cup (213 g) black beans

1 cup (164 g) corn kernels, canned or frozen

1 (10-oz [283-g]) can enchilada sauce

1 (2.25-oz [64-g]) can sliced black olives

12 corn tortillas

2 cups (240 g) shredded Mexican blend cheese, divided

Green onions, chopped, for garnish

Lettuce, shredded, for garnish

Mix together the meat, beans, corn, enchilada sauce and black olives. Place a double layer of tortillas in a 6-quart (6-L) slow cooker. Tear to make them fit if necessary. Top with half of the meat mixture. Sprinkle with half of the cheese. Repeat the process.

Cook on low for 3 hours or on high for 2 hours.

Serve immediately and garnish with green onions and lettuce.

MEXICAN RICE

This rice is easy to make and tastes better than the restaurant version. I used to go to the neighborhood Mexican restaurant to buy rice every time I made Mexican food but not anymore! This rice is the perfect addition to any Mexican menu and is the perfect base for Mexican Haystack (page 127).

SERVES 6 TO 8

2 tbsp (30 ml) vegetable or canola oil

1½ cups (316 g) long grain rice

½ cup (76 g) diced onion

¾ cup (177 ml) chicken broth

¾ cup (180 ml) tomato juice

1 (14.5-oz [411-g]) can petite cut tomatoes

1 (4.5-oz [127-g]) can green chilies

1 tsp chili powder

1 tsp cumin

½ tsp salt

Heat the oil in a pan over medium heat and add the rice and onion. Stir until the rice turns white and begins to brown, 2 to 3 minutes.

Add the rice to a 6-quart (6-L) slow cooker along with the broth, tomato juice, tomatoes, green chilies, chili powder, cumin and salt. Stir to combine.

Cook on high for 3 to 4 hours. Check after 2 hours for doneness. Continue cooking until all the liquid is absorbed and the rice is fluffy.

CHILI CILANTRO LIME CHICKEN

My favorite way to use this Chili Cilantro Lime Chicken is in enchiladas, but this is also delicious on a salad topped with cheese and tortilla strips. A restaurant that I used to frequent in Utah served a similar salad, and it is what I always ordered. You can also use this chicken in a burrito, a taco or just eat it as it is!

SERVES 8

2½ to 3 lb (1 to 1.5 kg) boneless, skinless chicken breasts

6 tbsp (90 ml) honey

5 tbsp (70 ml) fresh lime juice

2 tsp (6 g) garlic powder

1 (4.5-oz [127-g]) can chopped green chilies

1 cup (240 ml) green enchilada sauce

½ to ¾ tsp salt

2 tbsp (19 g) cornstarch

Combine all the ingredients except for the cornstarch in a 6-quart (6-L) slow cooker and cook on low for 3 hours.

Remove the chicken from the slow cooker, shred it into large chunks and return it to the sauce. If you want to thicken the sauce, add the cornstarch and cook for 30 minutes on high. Serve over rice, on a salad or in an enchilada or burrito.

QUESO FUNDIDO

My favorite Mexican restaurant serves the most amazing Queso Fundido. I dream about this stuff and order it every single time I'm there. Sometimes I share it. I decided I needed it in my life more often, so I came up with this make-at-home version that works perfectly in the slow cooker. The slow cooker keeps the cheese melted and at the right consistency for dipping. Just grab your favorite tortilla chip!

SERVES 6

4 cups (482 g) Monterey Jack cheese

1 tbsp (12 g) finely chopped jalapeño

2 tsp (7 g) fresh minced garlic

⅓ cup (2 g) cilantro, plus additional for garnish

1 tomato, chopped, for garnish

Spray a 4-quart (4-L) slow cooker with cooking spray.

Place all the ingredients except for the tomato into the slow cooker and toss. Cook on high for 1½ hours, stirring every 30 minutes.

If serving directly from the slow cooker, top with chopped tomato and additional cilantro.

You can also place the cooked cheese into an ovenproof dish and then place it under the broiler for a few minutes to crisp and brown up the top. Then garnish with tomato and cilantro.

CILANTRO BLACK BEANS

You'll never open a can of beans again after seeing how delicious and easy they are to make in the slow cooker. The beans are seasoned with garlic, cumin and cilantro and make the perfect addition to any Mexican-themed dinner.

SERVES 10 TO 12

1 lb (453 g) dry black beans, rinsed

3 cups (709 ml) chicken broth

3 cups (709 ml) tomato juice

2 tsp (6 g) fresh minced garlic

2 tsp (5 g) cumin

½ cup (2 g) cilantro, chopped

Salt and pepper to taste

Place the beans into a 6-quart (6-L) slow cooker.

Mix together the broth, juice, garlic and cumin, and pour it over the beans.

Cover and cook on low for 6 to 8 hours. Stir occasionally if possible. When done, stir in the cilantro and add salt and pepper to taste.

> **NOTE:** If you live in high altitude, you will need to soak the beans overnight in water before putting them in the slow cooker.

NO—FRY REFRIED BEANS

These No-Fry Refried Beans make the perfect addition to a burrito, a quesadilla or as a topping for nachos. I love to melt cheese on the top of a bowl full of these beans and serve it as a dip.

SERVES 8 TO 10

3 cups (600 g) dry pinto beans, rinsed

½ cup (76 g) diced onion

4 tsp (12 g) minced garlic

2 tsp (10 g) salt

1 tsp ground black pepper

1 tsp cumin

5 cups (1 L) water

4 cups (946 ml) chicken broth

1 (4.5-oz [127-g]) can green chilies, diced

Spray the inside of a 6-quart (6-L) slow cooker with cooking spray. Place all the ingredients in the slow cooker and stir to mix. Cook on high for 8 hours.

After the beans are done cooking (watch to make sure you don't need to add any extra liquid during the cooking time), strain the beans but reserve the liquid.

Mash the beans with a potato masher and add the extra liquid to get the consistency and texture you want. Add additional seasonings to taste.

> **NOTE:** If you live in high altitude, you will need to soak the beans overnight in water before putting them in the slow cooker.

SALSA VERDE CARNITAS

This recipe has been a family favorite of ours for years. When my children were in college, they probably made this dish more than any other. They learned early to love their slow cookers. Placing the shredded meat in the oven for a few minutes before serving will crisp up the edges and adds a wonderful texture to the meat.

SERVES 8 TO 10

3 lb (1.5 kg) pork butt or shoulder

2 cups (518 g) salsa verde, bottled or canned

1 cup (151 g) chopped onion

1 cup (237 ml) chicken broth

1 tsp cumin

1 tsp ground coriander

1 tsp dried oregano

¼ cup (1 g) fresh cilantro, chopped

Corn tortillas

Place the pork in a 6-quart (6-L) slow cooker.

In a bowl, mix together the salsa verde, onion, broth and seasonings. Pour the mixture over the meat and cook on low for 6 hours. Cook until the meat is tender and pulls apart easily.

Preheat the oven to 400°F (204°C).

Remove the meat from the slow cooker and pull it apart, creating 1- to 2-inch (2.5- to 5-cm) chunks. Remove the liquid from the slow cooker and reserve 2 cups (473 ml).

Place the 2 cups (473 ml) of liquid in a saucepan and over medium heat bring it to a boil, cooking until it's slightly thickened and reduced down, 3 to 4 minutes.

Place the meat on a baking sheet and roast it in the oven for 5 to 10 minutes or until the meat begins to brown and gets crispy on the edges.

Pour some of the thickened juices over the meat to make it moister, if desired. Sprinkle with cilantro.

Serve as a taco on tortillas or over rice.

MEXICAN STREET CORN DIP

This dip has all the flavors of traditional Mexican street corn but in the form of a dip. Add additional corn flavor by using tortilla chips for dipping, and control your heat by the amount of chili powder you add. Then just watch it disappear!

SERVES 8

8 oz (225 g) cream cheese, softened

½ cup (122 g) plain Greek yogurt

2 tsp (7 g) fresh minced garlic

¼ tsp salt

1 tsp cumin

¾ tsp chili powder

1 lime, juiced

2 cups (241 g) shredded pepper jack cheese, divided

2 tbsp (19 g) chopped small red onion

2 (15-oz [425-g]) cans corn, drained

Green onion, Cotija cheese and chili powder, for garnish

Place the cream cheese, Greek yogurt, garlic, salt, cumin, chili powder, lime juice and 1 cup (121 g) cheese into a blender and blend until smooth.

Stir in the red onion, remaining cheese and corn, and mix by hand.

Spray a 4-quart (4-L) slow cooker with cooking spray. Add the mixture to the slow cooker and cook on low for 2 to 3 hours or on high for 1½ hours.

Garnish with chopped green onion, Cotija cheese and an additional sprinkle of chili powder.

MEXICAN HAYSTACK

Mexican Haystack will quickly become everyone's favorite. It is the perfect way to use up leftovers and feed a crowd during the holidays. It uses the Spicy Mexican Beef (page 112), Mexican Rice (page 117) and Cilantro Black Beans (page 122), along with lots of other fun toppings. Pork Tinga with Pineapple (page 114), Chili Cilantro Lime Chicken (page 118) and Salsa Verde Carnitas (page 124) would work great too. Everyone can personalize it to their own tastes. Just set out bowls of all the toppings and let everyone create their own dinner!

SERVES 6 TO 8

Mexican Rice (page 117)

Cilantro Black Beans (page 122)

Spicy Mexican Beef (page 112)

Grated cheddar cheese

Sliced black olives

Sliced avocado

Cilantro, chopped

Chips, crushed

Favorite dressing or ½ cup (123 g) sour cream and 4 tbsp (64 g) salsa

Build your Mexican Haystack starting with a base of rice and beans. Add the beef and then garnish with desired toppings (cheese, olives, avocado, cilantro and chips). Add your favorite dressing.

4TH OF JULY

Summer just may be my favorite time to use my slow cooker. It is the perfect way to prepare a meal and not heat up the house! I also love the freedom it gives me. I pop something in the slow cooker in the morning, and then I don't have to worry about dinner for the rest of the day. I can head to work or out to play with the kids and enjoy my day and still have something ready for dinner when everyone's hungry.

We love hosting a neighborhood BBQ or potluck during the summer, and some of these recipes have become favorites with our neighbors over the years. My most requested potluck dish is Everyone's Favorite Baked Beans (page 137) because they truly are the best. My neighbors are still raving about the Bacon Mac and Cheese (page 133) I shared with them while developing the recipes for this cookbook. Take advantage of the summer veggies and make Roasted Summer Vegetables (page 141), and the Cheesy Chili Corn Cake (page 134) is the perfect side dish for any BBQ. Just watch the No Fire Required S'mores Brownies (page 140) disappear at your summer gathering.

BBQ BEEF BRISKET

My favorite way to cook brisket is in the slow cooker. This simple recipe starts with a rub of spices and some liquid smoke to give it that smoky flavor without having to use a smoker. After the brisket is cooked, smother it with your favorite BBQ sauce and pop it back in the slow cooker to allow the sauce to set up. It's the perfect addition to your summer BBQ or potluck. Serve it with all the fixings—Bacon Mac and Cheese (page 133) and Cheesy Chili Corn Cake (page 134).

SERVES 8

1 tsp cumin

¼ tsp cinnamon

1 tsp smoked paprika

1 tsp chili powder

1 tbsp (12 g) brown sugar

1 tsp salt

1 tsp pepper

1 (3½-lb [1.5-kg]) brisket

1 (6-oz [170-g]) can tomato paste

½ cup (118 ml) beef broth

½ tsp liquid smoke

BBQ sauce

Mix together the cumin, cinnamon, smoked paprika, chili powder, brown sugar, salt and pepper. Rub the mixture into both sides of the brisket and let it sit for 30 minutes.

Place the brisket into a 6-quart (6-L) slow cooker and cover with tomato paste on both sides. Add the beef broth and liquid smoke.

Cook on low for 6 to 7 hours or on high for 5 hours until the brisket is very tender and slices easily.

Slice across the grain and put the meat back into the cooker and cover with BBQ sauce. Let it cook on low for 30 to 40 minutes to allow the sauce to set up.

BACON
MAC AND CHEESE

This is pure comfort food and what dreams are made of. The combination of four different cheeses along with whipping cream makes for a creamy and delicious combo. My neighbors are still talking about this mac and cheese months after I shared it with them.

SERVES 8 TO 10

½ tsp black pepper

1 tsp dry mustard

1 tsp garlic salt

1 tsp onion powder

½ tsp paprika

1 tsp dried parsley

½ tsp dried oregano

½ tsp dried basil

1 cup (121 g) grated medium or sharp cheddar cheese

1 cup (121 g) grated Monterey Jack cheese

1 cup (121 g) grated mozzarella cheese

½ cup (90 g) grated Parmesan cheese

2 cups (473 ml) whipping cream

1 cup (236 ml) 2% milk

¼ cup (57 g) butter, melted

2 cups (232 g) dry elbow macaroni

6 slices bacon, cooked crisp

Mix together the spices and set aside. Mix together the cheeses. Spray a 6-quart (6-L) slow cooker with cooking spray.

Mix together the cream, milk, butter and the reserved spices, and pour it into the slow cooker.

Add the pasta and three-quarters of the cheese mixture, mixing to combine.

Cook on low for 2 hours.

Top with the remaining cheese and the bacon and cook for an additional 30 minutes. Test the pasta to make sure it is tender. Cook an additional 30 minutes if needed.

CHEESY CHILI CORN CAKE

Also referred to as corn pudding, Cheesy Chili Corn Cake is soft, sweet and has a little heat. The sweetness of the corn combined with the little kick from the chilies makes for a perfect combo. The flavor is amazing, and this is always a hit at any potluck or BBQ.

SERVES 8 TO 10

8 oz (250 g) cream cheese, softened

2 eggs, beaten

½ cup (96 g) sugar

16 oz (453 g) frozen white or yellow corn

1 (14-oz [398-ml]) can creamed corn

2 (4.5-oz [127-g]) cans diced green chilies

1 (8.5-oz [240-g]) box corn muffin mix

2 cups (241 g) Mexican blend cheese (combo of Monterey Jack, colby and cheddar)

1 cup (237 ml) whole milk

2 tbsp (29 g) butter, melted

½ tsp salt

1 tsp garlic powder

½ tsp pepper

Spray a 6-quart (6-L) slow cooker with cooking spray or line it with a liner. Beat together the cream cheese, eggs and sugar until smooth.

Add all of the other ingredients and stir to combine.

Pour it into the slow cooker and cook on high for 3 hours. Remove the lid for the last 30 minutes of cooking.

SMOKY BBQ RIBS

Cooking ribs in the slow cooker will change your life with this one little tip. Season the ribs first, and then place them under the broiler to brown before adding them to the slow cooker with the sauce. Then when they are done cooking, pop them under the broiler again with a coating of the remaining sauce. They are perfection!

SERVES 4 TO 5

1 tsp garlic salt

1 tsp onion powder

½ tsp black pepper

5 to 6 lb (2 to 2.5 kg) baby back ribs

1 cup (235 ml) ketchup

¼ cup (60 ml) honey

¼ cup (60 ml) Worcestershire sauce

2 tbsp (30 ml) white vinegar

⅛ tsp liquid smoke

1 tsp garlic powder

½ tsp mustard powder

½ tsp salt

Combine the garlic salt, onion powder and black pepper and sprinkle it on both sides of the ribs.

Place the ribs on a baking sheet and put it 6 inches (15 cm) under the broiler for about 10 minutes or until browned. Turn once.

Move the ribs into a 6-quart (6-L) slow cooker that has been lined or sprayed with cooking spray.

Mix together all of the remaining ingredients and brush or pour approximately two-thirds of the sauce over the ribs. Make sure both sides of the ribs are coated.

Cook on low for 4 to 5 hours or until tender.

Remove the ribs and brush them with the remaining sauce, and, if desired, place the ribs under the broiler for a few minutes to allow the sauce to set up, or just pour the remaining sauce over the ribs.

HAWAIIAN BBQ CHICKEN

We have a local Hawaiian restaurant near us and its Shoyu (soy sauce) chicken is always the first thing to sell out each day. I'm always so sad when I get there after it's sold out. This make-at-home version is just as delicious, though, and I don't have to be sad! Serve it with rice and a side of macaroni salad, just as they do in Hawaii.

SERVES 8

6 to 8 chicken thighs
1 cup (237 ml) soy sauce
1 cup (220 g) packed brown sugar
½ cup (118 ml) chicken broth
4 tsp (13 g) fresh minced garlic
1 tbsp (14 g) fresh minced ginger
2 tbsp (30 ml) honey
½ cup (76 g) chopped onion
2 tbsp (19 g) cornstarch
Green onions, for garnish

Place the chicken inside a 6-quart (6-L) slow cooker.

Mix together the soy sauce, brown sugar, broth, garlic, ginger, honey and onion. Pour it over the chicken and cook on low for 3 to 4 hours or until the chicken is tender and pulls apart with a fork.

When the chicken is done, shred it with a fork. Remove ½ cup (118 ml) of the remaining liquid, and stir in the cornstarch. Add the cornstarch mixture and the shredded chicken back in the slow cooker and stir. Cook for 30 minutes to allow the sauce to thicken.

Serve over rice, and garnish with sliced green onions.

EVERYONE'S FAVORITE BAKED BEANS

The original recipe bakes in the oven for 3 hours, which takes up a lot of oven time and space, so I took this family favorite and turned it into a slow cooker dish.

SERVES 10 TO 12

2 (28-oz [794-g]) cans pork and beans or baked beans
1 cup (151 g) chopped onion
3 tbsp (45 ml) Worcestershire sauce
1 cup (237 ml) ketchup
½ cup (110 g) packed brown sugar
1 green pepper, cut into rings

Spray a 6-quart (6-L) slow cooker with cooking spray or use a liner. Stir and combine all the ingredients except for the green pepper rings in the slow cooker. Then place the green pepper rings on top.

Bake on low for 3 hours and then remove the lid and allow it to cook for 1 hour. This will help the beans thicken up.

TRIPLE-BERRY COBBLER

I live in the Pacific Northwest, where fresh berries grow along the roadside. This cobbler is the perfect thing to make with all of those summer berries. You can enjoy cobbler all year round, though, by using frozen berries. Mix up your berry combination depending on what's in season and what you have on hand.

SERVES 6

1 cup (124 g) flour

2 tbsp (27 g) sugar

1 tsp baking powder

1 egg

¼ cup (60 ml) 2% milk

2 tbsp (29 g) butter, melted

1 cup (125 g) fresh or frozen raspberries, thawed

1 cup (150 g) fresh or frozen blueberries, thawed

1 cup (144 g) fresh or frozen blackberries, thawed

¼ cup (38 g) cornstarch

⅛ tsp salt

1 tsp lemon juice

Mix together the flour, sugar and baking powder. In another bowl, whisk together the egg, milk and butter. Add the egg mixture to the flour mixture and stir until moistened. This will create a thick batter.

Spray a 6-quart (6-L) slow cooker with cooking spray or line with a liner and spread the batter evenly on the bottom.

Mix the berries, cornstarch, salt and lemon juice together in a bowl. Layer this on top of the batter in the slow cooker.

Cook on high for 2 hours or until the batter is cooked through and the berries are hot and bubbly.

Serve with vanilla ice cream.

NO FIRE REQUIRED S'MORES BROWNIES

These No Fire Required S'mores Brownies have all the goodness of the real thing. To give the brownies a more authentic s'mores look, remove them from the slow cooker and place under the broiler to brown the marshmallows. Lining the slow cooker with foil allows for easy removal.

SERVES 12

1½ cups (135 g) graham cracker crumbs (about 10 sheets)

¾ cup (153 g) granulated sugar, divided

6 tbsp (90 g) butter

½ cup (110 g) packed brown sugar

½ cup (115 g) butter, melted

1 tsp vanilla

3 eggs

⅔ cup (73 g) unsweetened cocoa powder

1¼ cups (156 g) all-purpose flour

½ tsp baking powder

½ tsp salt

1 cup (180 g) semisweet chocolate chips

1½ cups (135 g) miniature marshmallows

1 (1.5-oz [43-g]) chocolate bar (I like to use Hershey's), broken into pieces

Spray a 6-quart (6-L) slow cooker with cooking spray. Line the slow cooker with a piece of foil large enough to extend halfway up the sides of the slow cooker. Spray the foil with cooking spray.

In a small bowl, add the graham cracker crumbs, ⅓ cup (57 g) of sugar and butter. Stir to combine and then spread it evenly onto the bottom of the slow cooker.

Mix together ½ cup (96 g) of granulated sugar, brown sugar and melted butter. Add the vanilla, eggs and cocoa powder.

Combine the flour, baking powder and salt, and add it to the sugar mixture. Fold in the chocolate chips.

Spread the mixture over the graham cracker layer in the slow cooker. Cook on low for 3 hours.

Remove the lid and place the marshmallows on top of the brownie. Cook for 30 minutes. Allow it to cool for about 15 minutes and then lift the foil to remove the brownies from the slow cooker.

Place the brownies on a cookie sheet and put it under the broiler to brown the marshmallows.

Push the chocolate bar pieces into the top of the brownie and serve with ice cream.

ROASTED SUMMER VEGETABLES

Roasted Summer Vegetables are the perfect side dish to just about any meal, especially in the summer, when you have lots of fresh vegetables out of the garden. After the vegetables have finished cooking in the slow cooker, you can place them on a baking sheet and place them under the broiler for a few minutes to get some char marks on them if you like. Just watch them closely so they don't burn.

SERVES 6

3 bell peppers, cut into large slices (I used orange, red and yellow, and cut each pepper into 8 pieces)

1 large sweet potato, peeled and cut into 1-inch (25-mm) cubes

1 zucchini, cut into 1-inch (25-mm) coins

1 yellow squash, cut into 1-inch (25-mm) coins

2 tbsp (30 ml) olive oil

4 to 5 tsp (13 to 16 g) fresh minced garlic

1 tsp herbs de Provence

½ tsp salt

Place the vegetables in a 6-quart (6-L) slow cooker. Drizzle them with the olive oil, garlic and herbs de Provence, and stir to coat.

Cook on high for 3 hours. Stir once an hour if possible.

Place the vegetables on a cookie sheet and put it under the broiler for a few minutes if char marks are desired.

KALUA PORK

When you are looking for something you can put in the slow cooker and let cook for hours and hours, this is it! This tender pork can cook on low for 8 to 10 hours. It has plenty of flavor, so you can serve it just as it is, or you can add your favorite sauce, like BBQ sauce, teriyaki sauce or sweet chili sauce, to it, too.

SERVES 8 TO 10

3 to 4 lb (1.5 to 2 kg) pork shoulder roast

1 tbsp (15 g) Hawaiian sea salt or Kosher salt

1 tbsp (15 ml) soy sauce

4 tsp (20 ml) Worcestershire sauce

1 tsp liquid smoke

2 tbsp (18 g) brown sugar

Place the pork in a 6-quart (6-L) slow cooker and sprinkle it with salt. Mix together the other ingredients and pour it over the pork.

Cook on low for 6 to 7 hours or until the meat is extremely tender and pulls apart easily. Serve over rice or on buns.

NOTE: A good rule of thumb for seasoning meat is 1 tablespoon (15 g) salt for every 4 pounds (2 kg) of meat.

BREAKFAST

When it comes to slow cooker recipes, breakfast is probably the most overlooked category. Making breakfast with my slow cooker when I have overnight company is one of my favorite ways to use it.

The Overnight Apple Cinnamon Oatmeal (page 146) and the Green Chili and Cheese Overnight Breakfast Casserole (page 152) are the perfect things to serve overnight guests. Prepare it the night before and wake up to a delicious breakfast. I also like to make up a batch of the Make-It-Your-Own Homemade Granola (page 157) and serve it along with some yogurt and fresh berries to let my guests make their own breakfast parfaits.

A Dutch Baby (page 148) topped with berries, lemon juice and powdered sugar is always my kids' favorite, and the Sun-Dried Tomato, Basil and Sausage Crustless Quiche (page 158) is the perfect thing to serve at a brunch.

OVERNIGHT APPLE CINNAMON OATMEAL

Wake up to the amazing smell of apples, cinnamon and breakfast all ready to go. Start the day with a delicious hot breakfast by prepping the night before. This recipe uses steel-cut oats, and please don't try substituting regular oats. I like to use a slow cooker liner with this recipe as it makes cleanup much easier! You can also use this recipe to make plain oatmeal by leaving out the apples and using more water instead of apple juice.

SERVES 4

2 cups (473 ml) 2% milk

1 cup (237 ml) water

1½ cups (355 ml) apple juice

1 cup (161 g) steel-cut oats

2 tbsp (29 g) butter

½ tsp salt

¼ cup (60 ml) maple syrup

1 tsp vanilla

¼ tsp nutmeg

2 tsp (5 g) cinnamon

2 cups (235 g) diced Granny Smith apples

Use a slow cooker liner or spray the inside of a 6-quart (6-L) slow cooker with cooking spray. Mix together all the ingredients and place them in the slow cooker.

Cook on low for 8 hours or overnight.

Remove the lid for 20 to 30 minutes to allow it to thicken, if needed.

CORNED BEEF HASH

This is the perfect way to use up any leftover corned beef (from Reuben Sandwich, page 174). I like to use leftover potatoes in my hash, too, as the chilled potatoes hold their shape better when cooking.

SERVES 4

2 tbsp (30 ml) olive oil

½ cup (76 g) chopped onion

4 to 5 red potatoes, cooked, cubed and chilled

1 tsp garlic powder

½ cup (90 g) diced red pepper

2 cups (470 g) shredded or cubed corned beef

¼ tsp oregano

Salt and pepper to taste

4 eggs, cooked to taste

In a large frying pan, heat up the olive oil and sauté the onion for a few minutes until it begins to soften. Add the potatoes, garlic powder and red pepper, and cook until the potatoes are browned, 4 to 5 minutes.

Add the corned beef and oregano and stir to heat through. Salt and pepper to taste.

Cook eggs as desired and place on top of individual servings of the hash.

DUTCH BABY

A Dutch Baby, or puff-up pancake, as my kids like to call it, is definitely a favorite breakfast at our house. We like to eat it topped with fresh berries, sprinkled with powdered sugar and drizzled with lemon juice.

SERVES 4 TO 6

4 tbsp (58 g) melted butter

1 cup (125 g) flour

1 cup (237 ml) milk

6 eggs

½ tsp salt

¼ tsp baking powder

1 tbsp (12 g) sugar

1 tsp vanilla

Powdered sugar and lemon juice, for garnish

Spray the inside of a 6-quart (6-L) slow cooker with cooking spray. Pour the butter into the bottom of the slow cooker. Mix together the remaining ingredients, except the powdered sugar and lemon juice, and pour it into the slow cooker.

Cover the top of the slow cooker with a paper towel or cotton towel and put on the lid. Cook for about 1 to 1½ hours or until the egg is cooked through. Cut into individual servings and sprinkle with powdered sugar and drizzle with lemon juice.

BREAKFAST POTATOES WITH PEPPERS

The addition of red peppers and jalapeños to these potatoes not only adds lots of great flavor, but spice too. We like using red peppers, but you can substitute your favorite pepper. Removing the lid for the last 30 minutes of cooking will give the potatoes a chance to crisp up on top.

SERVES 6 TO 8

3 tbsp (45 g) butter

1 diced red pepper

1 jalapeño, diced small for additional heat, if desired

½ cup (76 g) diced onion

2 tsp (7 g) fresh minced garlic

3 tbsp (23 g) flour

1 cup (237 ml) 2% milk

1 cup (120 g) sour cream

1½ tsp (7 g) salt

½ tsp pepper

30 oz (850 g) frozen shredded hash browns, thawed

1 cup (121 g) freshly grated pepper jack cheese

Green onion, chopped, diced bacon and additional cheese, for garnish

In a pan, melt the better and add the peppers, onion and garlic. Sauté over medium heat until tender, about 5 minutes. Reduce heat to low and add the flour and stir until a thick roux forms. Slowly add the milk, stirring continuously. Remove the pan from the heat and stir in the sour cream. Add the salt and pepper.

Spray a 6-quart (6-L) slow cooker with cooking spray and add the thawed hash browns and cheese. Cover with the pepper mixture and stir to combine.

Cover and cook on high for 2 to 3 hours. Remove the lid for the last 30 minutes to allow the potatoes to crisp up a bit on top. If you prefer a crisper potato, place the potatoes in an oven-safe pan and then put it under the broiler for a minute or two before serving.

Garnish with green onion, diced bacon or more cheese!

CINNAMON SALTED CARAMEL AND WALNUT MONKEY BREAD

This sweet, gooey and nutty monkey bread will be the most popular dish at your brunch or breakfast. Using refrigerated biscuits makes this so easy to put together. Be sure to use the towel trick to keep the bread from getting soggy from the condensation that collects on the slow cooker lid.

SERVES 4 TO 6

1 (16.3-oz [453-g]) tube refrigerated biscuits, jumbo size (8 biscuits)

½ cup (96 g) granulated sugar

1 tsp cinnamon

¼ cup (57 g) butter, melted

½ cup (110 g) packed brown sugar

¼ cup (29 g) chopped walnuts

Dulce de Leche sauce (page 69) or caramel sauce of choice

Large flake sea salt

Line a 6-quart (6-L) slow cooker with parchment paper, or to prevent the biscuits from overcooking on the edges, create a foil liner for the slow cooker. Use two pieces of foil that are 18 inches (45.5 cm) long. Fold in half and then fold again so that each foil piece measures 4 × 18 inches (10 × 45.5 cm) long. Place both pieces into the slow cooker so that they line the sides of the slow cooker. Then place a piece of parchment paper inside the slow cooker, over the foil.

Cut the biscuits into quarters. Mix together the granulated sugar and cinnamon and place it in a large plastic baggie. Add the cut biscuit pieces and toss to coat.

Place the biscuit pieces in the bottom of the slow cooker in a single layer. Mix together the melted butter and brown sugar. Drizzle it over the biscuit pieces and sprinkle with the remaining sugar from the plastic baggie. Sprinkle the biscuits with walnuts.

Place a cotton towel or paper towel between the lid and cooker to absorb the condensation and prevent the monkey bread from getting soggy.

Cook for 1½ hours on high. If the middle of the biscuits are still undercooked, cook for 5 more minutes and check for doneness. Repeat until they are cooked through.

Drizzle with caramel sauce and sea salt. Serve warm.

GREEN CHILI AND CHEESE OVERNIGHT BREAKFAST CASSEROLE

This is the perfect dish to serve to overnight guests or on a holiday morning. Put it all in the slow cooker right before going to bed, and breakfast will be ready when you wake up. I have tried using cubed hash browns but thought they got too mushy, so I prefer the grated hash browns. You can dress this up as much as you want by adding other fun flavors like some chopped red pepper or other veggies.

SERVES 6

1 (26-oz [737-g]) bag frozen shredded hash brown potatoes, divided

12 eggs, beaten

1 cup (237 ml) 2% milk

1 tsp garlic powder

1 tsp salt

½ tsp pepper

1 cup (151 g) chopped onion, divided

1 (16-oz [453-g]) package ground breakfast sausage, cooked and drained, divided

8 slices bacon, cooked crisp and chopped, divided

2 (4.5-oz [133-g]) cans green chilies, divided

3 cups (362 g) Mexican blend grated cheese, divided

Salsa, for garnish

Spray a 6-quart (6-L) slow cooker with cooking spray. Place half of the hash browns in the bottom of the slow cooker.

Whisk together the eggs, milk, garlic powder, salt and pepper.

Sprinkle half of the onion, sausage, bacon, one can of green chilies and half of the cheese over the hash browns. Repeat layers, starting with hash browns and ending with cheese.

Pour the egg mixture over the cheese.

Cook on low for 7 to 8 hours. If the potatoes were thawed, cook for 6 to 7 hours.

DENVER OMELET STRATA

A strata is similar to a quiche or a frittata but has a layer of bread. This dish has all the popular flavors of a Denver omelet but in strata form. It's a perfect dish for a holiday breakfast or brunch, and your friends will think you are fancy for making a strata! I love using pepper jack cheese for an extra kick, but feel free to use your favorite cheese or cheese blend.

SERVES 4 TO 6

Half of a 14-oz (396-g) loaf of French bread, cut into large cubes

1 cup (175 g) diced red pepper

½ cup (76 g) diced onion

2 tbsp (29 g) butter

9 eggs

1 cup (237 ml) 2% milk

1 tsp salt

½ tsp pepper

½ tsp garlic powder

1 cup (150 g) cubed ham

1½ cups (181 g) pepper jack cheese, divided

2 to 3 green onions, sliced, for garnish

Preheat the oven to 250°F (121°C).

I like to use a liner for this dish so that I can easily remove it from the slow cooker and put it on a pretty plate. Be sure to spray your liner with cooking spray. If you're not using a liner, spray the inside of the slow cooker well.

Place the cubed bread on a baking sheet and put it in the oven for about 15 minutes to allow the bread to dry out.

Place the bread in the bottom of a 6-quart (6-L) slow cooker.

Sauté the red peppers and onions in butter over medium heat until they begin to soften, 2 to 3 minutes.

Mix together the eggs, milk, salt, pepper and garlic powder. Add the ham, pepper and onion mixture and 1 cup (130 g) of cheese.

Pour the egg mixture over the bread in the slow cooker. Place a paper towel or cotton towel over the top of the cooker, under the lid, to absorb moisture, and cook on low for 3½ hours.

During the last 30 minutes, add the remaining cheese on top. Garnish with green onions.

BANANAS FOSTER FRENCH TOAST

This stuff is amazing! It actually tastes more like dessert than breakfast, but I'm a total fan of dessert for breakfast. The secret to great slow cooker French toast is to toast the bread before putting it in the slow cooker. It keeps the bread from getting too mushy. The sauce is added to the French toast after it is done cooking. I like using French bread with a softer crust rather than a thick, crispy artisan crust. Start the slow cooker when you wake up and by the time the rest of the family is up, you'll have a delicious dessert, I mean breakfast, to serve them!

SERVES 4 TO 6

1-lb (454-g) loaf French bread, cut into 1-inch (25-mm) cubes

7 eggs

2 cups (473 ml) 2% milk

¼ cup (59 ml) maple syrup

2 tsp (9 g) vanilla

1 tsp cinnamon

SAUCE

6 tbsp (86 g) butter

¾ cup (165 g) brown sugar

Pinch of salt

2 tbsp (30 ml) corn syrup

¼ cup (59 ml) whipping cream

1½ tsp (7 ml) vanilla

2 to 3 bananas, sliced

Preheat the oven to 250°F (122°C).

Place the cubed bread on a baking sheet and bake in the oven for about 20 minutes or until the bread is crispy on the outside (not browned).

Place the bread in a 6-quart (6-L) slow cooker lined with parchment paper or a liner bag.

Combine the eggs, milk, maple syrup, vanilla and cinnamon, and pour it over the bread. Stir to coat the bread, so that the majority of the milk is absorbed.

Place a cotton towel or a double layer of paper towels between the slow cooker and the lid to absorb the condensation that forms on the lid and prevent it from running onto the bread. Cook on high for 2 hours.

To make the sauce, melt the butter in a saucepan over medium heat and add the brown sugar, salt and corn syrup. Cook and stir until the sugar is melted and the sauce is smooth, about 2 to 3 minutes. Bring it to a boil. Add the whipping cream, remove the pan from the heat and add the vanilla. Stir in the sliced bananas and pour the sauce over the French toast.

MAKE-IT-YOUR-OWN HOMEMADE GRANOLA

Granola is not only for breakfast. I love to keep a container of it around just for snacking. I am also not opposed to sprinkling it over a bowl of ice cream or yogurt. Granola is so versatile! This is a good basic recipe for homemade granola that you can adapt to your own personal nut and fruit preferences. You can even divide the granola into smaller containers and let each family member *make it their own* by adding their favorite combination of fruit and nuts.

MAKES 5 TO 6 CUPS (850 TO 1,022 G)

4 cups (322 g) old-fashioned oats

¼ cup (55 g) brown sugar

2 tbsp (30 ml) honey

¼ tsp salt

¼ cup (59 ml) canola or coconut oil

1 cup (125 g) nuts
(pecans, walnuts, almonds)

1 to 2 cups (160 to 320 g) dried fruit

Spray the bottom of a 6-quart (6-L) slow cooker with cooking spray.

Place the oats in the slow cooker. Mix together the brown sugar, honey, salt and oil. Pour it over the oats and stir to coat.

Cook on high for 1 to 2 hours. Be sure to leave the lid slightly ajar so the granola doesn't get soggy. Stir every 20 to 30 minutes to prevent burning. The granola will become toasted and golden brown.

Remove the granola from the slow cooker and spread it in a single layer on a baking sheet and allow it to cool.

Add your favorite nut and fruit combination.

SUN-DRIED TOMATO, BASIL AND SAUSAGE CRUSTLESS QUICHE

Quiche is one of my favorite dishes to serve company for breakfast or lunch. This quiche has no crust but still has all the flavor and goodness you are used to in a quiche. It is also a great way to use up some of the leftovers in your fridge. This version uses sun-dried tomatoes, basil and sausage, but feel free to make it your own and switch them out for what you have on hand. Try using ham with some leftover veggies and some pepper jack cheese. Imagine the possibilities!

SERVES 6 TO 8

½ lb (227 g) mild Italian sausage

½ cup (76 g) diced onion

8 large eggs

1 cup (236 ml) half-and-half

2 cups (241 g) freshly shredded mozzarella cheese

⅓ cup (35 g) oil-packed sun-dried tomatoes, rinsed and chopped

½ cup (76 g) diced onion

⅓ cup (2 g) cut and loosely packed fresh basil

1 tsp salt

¼ tsp pepper

¼ cup (45 g) grated Parmesan cheese

In a pan, cook the sausage over medium heat until cooked through, about 5 minutes. Halfway through the cooking process, add the onions and allow them to soften.

Line a 6-quart (6-L) slow cooker with parchment paper.

In a bowl, mix together all the ingredients, including the sausage mixture, except for the Parmesan cheese.

Pour the mixture into the lined slow cooker and sprinkle with Parmesan cheese.

Place a cotton towel or paper towel over the slow cooker and then put on the lid. Make sure the towel is pulled tightly so it doesn't touch the egg mixture.

Cook on high for 3 to 4 hours or until the eggs are set and cooked through.

Using the parchment paper, lift the quiche out of the slow cooker and allow it to cool for 15 minutes before serving.

SANDWICHES AND STARTERS

I have some major sports fans at my house. They love their baseball, basketball, football, golf . . . you name it! Almost as important to them as whether their favorite team wins or not is what there is to eat while they watch their game.

The recipes in this section are perfect game-watching food but are also great for any day or night of the week. The Tri-Tip Sandwich with Chipotle Mayo (page 176) quickly became a favorite at our house, and I love that you can serve it a few different ways. The Cuban Pork Sandwich (page 170), the Smoky Chipotle Sloppy Joes (page 175) and the Reuben Sandwich with Russian Dressing (page 174) will all become favorites and make the perfect weekly family dinner ideal too.

If you are looking for some dip to put that chip into, my all-time favorite dip is the Roasted Garlic Artichoke Dip (page 169) but the Chicken Enchilada Dip (page 167) is a close second.

KUNG PAO CHICKEN WINGS

These wings have all the flavors of traditional Chinese stir-fry but in a fun,
"eat it with your fingers" form. They are savory and spicy thanks to the red
chili flakes, and they're topped with chopped peanuts and onion.

SERVES 6 TO 8

3 to 4 lb (1.5 to 2 kg) chicken wings

Salt and pepper to taste

½ cup (118 ml) chicken broth

½ cup (118 ml) soy sauce

¼ cup (59 ml) rice vinegar

¼ cup (36 g) brown sugar

½ tsp sesame oil

1 tbsp (15 ml) hoisin sauce

4 tsp (134 g) fresh minced garlic

1 tsp fresh minced ginger

1 tsp red chili flakes

2 tbsp (19 g) cornstarch

2 tbsp (30 ml) water

¼ cup (30 g) finely chopped peanuts, for garnish

Green onions, for garnish

Place the chicken wings in a 6-quart (6-L) slow cooker and season with salt and pepper.

Combine the broth, soy sauce, rice vinegar, brown sugar, oil, hoisin sauce, garlic, ginger and red chili flakes in a bowl.

Pour it over the chicken in the slow cooker and cook on low for 4 hours.

Combine the cornstarch and water.

When the chicken is done, drain and reserve the liquid. Place the liquid into a saucepan and add the cornstarch mixture. Stir it and bring it to a boil; cook it until it begins to thicken, about 5 minutes.

Place the chicken on a foil-lined baking pan and baste it with the thickened sauce mixture. Place it under the broiler and broil until the edges begin to brown and turn crispy, about 3 to 4 minutes. Turn the chicken, baste and broil again.

Garnish with the chopped peanuts and green onion.

HONEY SESAME CHICKEN WINGS

Whether served as an appetizer or as a meal, these Honey Sesame Chicken Wings are a crowd-pleaser and a favorite of the men in my house for their football-watching parties. I like to pop them under the broiler after they are done cooking to get them a little crispy around the edges. The sweetness of these wings is a perfect complement to the heat of the Kung Pao Chicken Wings (page 162).

SERVES 6 TO 8

⅓ cup (78 ml) chicken broth

⅓ cup (78 ml) soy sauce

1 tbsp (15 g) oyster sauce

1 tbsp (15 ml) rice wine vinegar

1 tsp fresh minced ginger

½ tbsp (7 ml) sesame oil

½ cup (118 ml) honey

4 tsp (13 g) fresh minced garlic

3 lb (1.5 kg) chicken wings

2 tbsp (19 g) cornstarch

2 tbsp (30 ml) water

Sesame seeds and green onion, for garnish

In a bowl, combine the chicken broth, soy sauce, oyster sauce, red wine vinegar, ginger, sesame oil, honey and garlic.

Place the chicken wings in a 6-quart (6-L) slow cooker. Cover the chicken with the sauce and cook on low for 3 to 4 hours.

In a small bowl, combine the cornstarch and water.

Drain and reserve the sauce from the chicken, place the sauce in a small pan and add the cornstarch mixture. Stir and bring it to a boil. Cook for 5 to 10 minutes.

Baste the chicken wings with the thickened sauce and place them under the broiler until they begin to brown and crisp on the edges, 3 to 4 minutes.

Turn the chicken wings and baste the other side. Broil until they are crispy on the edges.

Serve topped with sesame seeds and diced green onion.

BUFFALO CHICKEN MEATBALLS

I don't think any sports-watching event would be complete without buffalo chicken in some form. They just go together. These meatballs are a fun twist on a classic flavor combination. You can control your heat by the amount of hot sauce you put in. Substitute more ketchup and less hot sauce if you want a lower heat rating.

SERVES 4 TO 6

1 lb (454 kg) ground chicken
½ cup (90 g) fine bread crumbs
1 egg
2 tsp (6 g) fresh minced garlic
1 tsp dried minced onion
½ tsp salt
2 green onions, chopped fine
½ cup (118 ml) hot sauce
½ cup (118 ml) chicken broth
¼ cup (59 ml) ketchup

Preheat the oven to 400°F (209°C).

Mix together the chicken, bread crumbs, egg, garlic, onion, salt and green onions.

Form the mixture into meatballs, about 1½ inches (4 cm) in size. Place the meatballs on a parchment-lined baking sheet and bake for about 5 minutes or until they're lightly browned. This will help the meatballs hold their shape in the slow cooker.

Place the meatballs in a 6-quart (6-L) slow cooker. Mix together the hot sauce, broth and ketchup, and pour it over the meatballs. Stir to coat.

Cook on low for 2 hours.

CHICKEN ENCHILADA DIP

Enchiladas are my favorite Mexican food, and I love being able to enjoy one of my favorites in appetizer form, too. This one is a crowd-pleaser. You can use leftover chicken for this dip if you have it on hand, or cook up a chicken breast just for the dip, but don't leave it out! Enjoy all the flavors of an enchilada on a chip!

SERVES 6 TO 8

1 chicken breast (about 2 cups [250 g], shredded)

1 tbsp (3 g) taco seasoning

8 oz (225 g) cream cheese, softened

½ cup (60 g) sour cream

½ cup (110 g) mayo

1 (10-oz [283-g]) can diced tomatoes with green chilies (I like to use Rotel)

½ cup (120 ml) red enchilada sauce

1 (4.5-oz [127-g]) can diced green chilies

1 cup (121 g) grated Monterey Jack cheese

Grated cheese, cilantro and black olives, for garnish

Preheat the oven to 350°F (177°C).

Sprinkle the chicken breast with taco seasoning and bake in the oven for about 15 minutes or until cooked through. Shred the chicken.

In a bowl, beat the cream cheese until smooth. Add the sour cream, mayo, tomatoes, enchilada sauce and green chilies. Stir in the cheese.

Put the mixture in a 4-quart (4-L) slow cooker and cook on high for 1 to 2 hours or until it's heated through.

Top with additional grated cheese, cilantro and black olives. Serve with tortilla chips.

CHEESY BEAN DIP

This recipe is one that has been in my collection for years. It was handwritten by a friend years ago on a piece of fruit-bordered stationery. The only problem is, there is no name on the recipe, and I can't remember who gave this gem to me. I do remember how delicious it is, though. Whenever you share a recipe with a friend, be sure to put your name on it!

SERVES 8

8 oz (225 g) cream cheese, softened

1 (16-oz [454–g]) can refried beans

1 cup (120 g) sour cream

1 (1.25-oz [35-g]) package taco seasoning mix

1 (4.5-oz [127-g)] can diced green chilies

1 (16-oz [454-g]) jar green chili salsa

1 cup (121 g) grated Monterey Jack cheese

Mix together the cream cheese, beans, sour cream, taco seasoning, green chilies and green chili salsa, and place them in a 4-quart (4-L) slow cooker. Sprinkle the top with grated cheese.

Cook for about 1½ hours on high. The dip is done when it is heated through, bubbly around the edges and the cheese is melted.

ROASTED GARLIC ARTICHOKE DIP

This may be my favorite appetizer of all time and my most requested one. The addition of roasted garlic is what takes this dip to the top. Also, cooking it in a slow cooker gives you a nice, smooth consistency, and I love the crispy edges that form in the slow cooker. I think I may like the slow cooker version better than the one I make in the oven.

SERVES 6 TO 8

8 oz (225 g) cream cheese, softened

½ cup (60 g) sour cream

½ cup (110 g) mayonnaise

1 cup (180 g) Parmesan cheese

1 (6.5-oz [170-g]) jar artichoke hearts, drained and finely chopped

½ cup (60 g) shredded Monterey Jack cheese

¼ tsp pepper

1 head Roasted Garlic (page 40)

In a bowl, mix together all the ingredients. Spray a 4-quart (4-L) slow cooker with cooking spray and spread the dip evenly in the cooker.

Cook on high for 1½ hours or until the dip is heated through and bubbly and brown around the edges.

Serve with sliced French bread or crackers.

CUBAN PORK SANDWICH

I had my first Cuban pork sandwich at a restaurant in Seattle, and I dreamed about that sandwich for months afterward. Coming up with a version I could make at home became a top priority, and this recipe is the result. Serve this pork on a ciabatta roll or other chewy roll.

SERVES 6 TO 8

3 lb (1.5 kg) boneless pork shoulder or picnic roast

7 tsp (23 g) fresh minced garlic

2 tsp (5 g) black pepper

2 tsp (5 g) salt

1 cup (237 ml) fresh squeezed orange juice

½ cup (118 ml) fresh squeezed lime juice

3 tbsp (40 g) dark brown sugar

1 tsp dried oregano

½ tsp cumin

1 cup (151 g) diced onion

2 bay leaves

GARLIC MAYO

2 tbsp (20 g) fresh minced garlic

¼ tsp garlic salt

1 cup (220 g) mayo

3 tbsp (45 g) sweet relish

1 tsp fresh squeezed lemon juice

Place the pork in a 6-quart (6-L) slow cooker.

Combine the garlic, pepper, salt, juices, sugar, spices, onion and bay leaves in a bowl. Pour it over the pork in the slow cooker.

Cook on low for 7 to 8 hours or until tender and the pork pulls apart easily. Remove the pork from the slow cooker, tear it into large pieces and remove the bay leaves.

Add the pork back to the liquid in the slow cooker and allow it to absorb the liquid. Keep it warm until you are ready to serve it.

To make the garlic mayo, combine all of the ingredients. Spread it on a chewy roll and top with the pork. Be generous with the spread. Refrigerate the garlic mayo until ready to serve.

RASPBERRY BALSAMIC CHILI MEATBALLS

I had a roommate in college who could cook one thing and it was chicken covered in grape jelly and chili sauce. At the time, I thought it was a very strange combination. I'm not kidding when I say she could cook *one* thing, as she made this over and over again. Much to my surprise, it was a yummy combination, and I found myself making it throughout the years! This recipe is my slightly more sophisticated version of her grape jelly chicken.

SERVES 8

2 lb (1 kg) hamburger

1 cup (180 g) fine bread crumbs

2 eggs

1 tsp salt

½ tsp pepper

1 cup (325 g) raspberry jam

1 cup (245 g) chili sauce

2 tbsp (30 ml) honey

⅓ cup (80 ml) balsamic vinegar

Preheat the oven to 400°F (204°C).

Spray a 6-quart (6-L) slow cooker with cooking spray.

Mix together the hamburger, bread crumbs, eggs, salt and pepper. Form it into 1½-inch (4-cm) meatballs, and place them on a parchment-lined baking sheet. Bake in the oven for 5 minutes or until they begin to brown. The meatballs do not need to be cooked through.

Place the meatballs in the slow cooker.

Mix together the jam, chili sauce, honey and balsamic vinegar, and pour it over the meatballs.

Bake on low for 2 hours and check to make sure the hamburger is cooked through.

Stir several times during the cooking process to coat the meatballs with the sauce.

REUBEN SANDWICH WITH RUSSIAN DRESSING

The inspiration for this recipe came from my continual craving for a sandwich we had eaten at a deli in Santa Barbara, California, on a recent road trip. It was one of those restaurants/diners where you sit at the counter and watch the cook do his thing. The sandwich was amazing, and I couldn't wait to recreate it at home. You can serve it on rye bread for a more traditional Reuben, but I prefer toasted sourdough bread. A true Reuben is also served with sauerkraut, which I am not crazy about, but if you like it, top your corned beef with some when putting your sandwich together. Be sure to save some of the corned beef for some Corned Beef Hash (page 148). Corned beef comes in a point cut or a flat cut. Point cut is better for shredding, so that is what I use. If you prefer to slice your corned beef, use the flat cut.

SERVES 6 TO 8

RUSSIAN DRESSING

½ cup (110 g) mayo

1 tsp dried minced onion

1 tsp fresh minced garlic

1 tsp Worcestershire sauce

1 tsp dried parsley

2 tbsp (31 g) chili sauce

2 tbsp (31 g) ketchup

2 to 3 lb (1 to 1.5 kg) corned beef brisket with spice packet, point cut

1 tsp whole peppercorns

Rye bread or sourdough bread, toasted

6 to 8 slices Swiss cheese

Sauerkraut, optional

To make the Russian dressing, combine the mayo, onion, garlic, Worcestershire sauce, parsley, chili sauce and ketchup. Stir and refrigerate until you're ready to use it.

Trim the fat from the corned beef brisket. Place the meat in a 6-quart (6-L) slow cooker.

Sprinkle it with the spice packet and peppercorns, and add enough water to cover the brisket.

Cook on low for 6 to 8 hours or on high for 3 to 4 hours. The meat should be very tender and shred easily with two forks or slice easily across the grain.

To make the sandwich, I like to add a little oil to a pan and fry the shredded brisket for a few minutes to get the edges crisp, but this is totally optional.

Toast the bread and spread it with the Russian dressing. Top the bread with the corned beef, add the cheese and place the open-faced sandwich under the broiler to melt the cheese. If you are frying it in a pan, add the cheese while the meat is in the pan, turn off the burner and cover the pan with a lid to allow the cheese to melt. Add the meat and cheese to the toasted bread that is spread with Russian dressing and top it with sauerkraut if you'd like.

SMOKY CHIPOTLE SLOPPY JOES

Sloppy joes were on the weekly dinner rotation when I was a kid, but they were generally made with ground hamburger and ketchup. We've grown up a bit since then, and so have sloppy joes. The chipotle peppers and red peppers give these a more grown-up taste that even the kids will love.

SERVES 6 TO 8

3 lb (1.5 kg) boneless chuck roast cut into 1½-inch (4-cm) pieces

1 cup (151 g) chopped onions

1 cup (175 g) chopped red bell pepper

1½ cups (368 g) ketchup

4 tbsp (65 g) tomato paste

2 chipotle peppers, minced, with juice

1 tsp chili powder

1 tsp cumin

1 tsp garlic powder

4 tbsp (47 g) sugar

1 tbsp (15 ml) white vinegar

Place the meat pieces, onion and peppers into a 6-quart (6-L) slow cooker.

Mix together all the remaining ingredients, and pour them over the meat mixture. Stir to combine.

Cook on low for 4 hours or on high for 6 hours or until the meat shreds easily.

Shred the meat and stir it into the juices in the slow cooker. Allow it to sit in the slow cooker for 30 minutes so that the juices can absorb into the meat before serving.

TRI-TIP SANDWICH WITH CHIPOTLE MAYO

This tri-tip sandwich is sure to be a people pleaser. You can serve it two ways. The first is as a French dip sandwich. Add cheese and use the delicious juices leftover as a dipping sauce. I also like to add some chipotle mayo to mine. If you prefer a Philly cheesesteak–style sandwich, just sauté some peppers and onions and add them to the sandwich along with the cheese.

SERVES 4 TO 6

1 tsp sea salt

½ tsp pepper

½ tsp dried thyme leaves

½ tsp dried rosemary leaves

2 tsp (6 g) fresh minced garlic

1 (3-lb [1.5-kg]) tri-tip roast

2 cups (473 ml) beef broth

2 tbsp (30 ml) Worcestershire sauce

6 slices provolone cheese

Buns, for serving

CHIPOTLE MAYO

½ cup (110 g) mayonnaise

1 tsp adobe sauce from chipotle peppers

1 to 2 chipotle chilies in adobo sauce

Combine the salt, pepper, thyme, rosemary and garlic, and rub it over the top of the tri-tip. Place the meat into a 6-quart (6-L) slow cooker.

Add the broth and Worcestershire sauce to the slow cooker around the sides of the meat. Do not pour directly over the top of the tri-tip and wash off the seasoning.

Cook on low for 6 to 7 hours or until the meat is tender and pulls apart easily with a fork.

Remove the meat from the slow cooker and shred it into large pieces. Strain the remaining liquid and use it as a dip for the sandwich.

For the chipotle mayo, combine the mayonnaise, adobe sauce and chipotle chilies, and refrigerate until it's ready to use.

Spread the chipotle mayo on a toasted bun, top with the meat and cheese. Place it under the broiler for a minute to melt the cheese.

If you prefer a Philly cheesesteak–style sandwich, sauté some onions and peppers in 2 tablespoons (30 ml) canola or olive oil over medium-high heat until soft, about 5 minutes, and add this to the sandwich along with the provolone cheese.

ACKNOWLEDGMENTS

To Jim, my biggest cheerleader, number one taste tester and tireless dishwasher: For 35 years you have supported me, encouraged me and weathered dozens of reach-for-the-stars ideas and projects. When I decided to start a blog (with no idea how to do it) you just smiled. When you walk in the door after work to a kitchen full of dishes, you just get to work washing. You may shake your head every now and then at the craziness of it all, but you are an unfailing anchor amid the chaos. This cookbook and my blog wouldn't have been possible without you.

To Logan, Clark, Cali and Tessa, my four children: You have grown into amazing adults and make me proud every day. You were there in the beginning, when my culinary abilities hadn't quite . . . blossomed . . . yet. When all I put on the table week after week was BBQ chicken wings and Boboli pizza. Now I love visiting you in your homes and having you cook for me! You are much better cooks than I ever was at your age.

To Mom and Dad: Thanks for loving me and supporting me, always. Mom—you are a wonderful cook and some of my favorite recipes are ones you made for us growing up. Readers will find variations of some of them here in the cookbook. I know Dad is cheering me on from heaven and I wish he could taste some of the yummy things found on these pages.

To my neighbors (or my second family): Thank you for always being willing to taste test my recipes—both those in this cookbook as well as those on the blog. Your sweet texts telling me how delicious things were made my heart sing! Thank you for letting us borrow your children, now that we are empty nesters, and for coming to our parties. You are truly our family. Thanks to your willingness to take extra food off our hands, so Jim and I don't weigh three times as much as we do!

To my blog readers: Thank you for your encouragement and for the question you dared to ask that sparked all of this: "When are you going to write a cookbook?" I'm glad I finally gave in and decided to do it. Thank you for taking the time to email, comment, share and stop me in the halls of conferences to tell me about how my recipes have helped and blessed your life. It's those interactions that keep me blogging.

To my amazing team at Page Street: Thank you for inviting me to write this cookbook and for your support, guidance and encouragement throughout the entire process. It may have been one of the most difficult work projects I have ever taken on, but it is also one of the most rewarding. Thank you for the opportunity.

To my talented food photographers and stylists, Erica and Bri: You girls are simply a delight! The week we spent together photographing, eating, playing in the snow and enjoying ice cream were a highlight of this entire process. You captured my recipes beautifully. I can't wait to work together again.

To my fellow blogger, friend and kindred spirit, Mary: Thank you for your guidance and encouragement throughout this entire cookbook-writing process. Being able to talk it through with you, ask questions, quell my fears and get your sage advice made all the difference in my decision to go forward with this. You and others like you in the blogging world inspire, uplift and encourage me to reach higher than I ever thought possible.

To all my wonderful recipe testers: Thank you so much for your effort, feedback, ideas and suggestions. I couldn't have done this without you!

ABOUT THE AUTHOR

Leigh Anne Wilkes is that neighbor you love. You know the one—they throw amazing parties, they bring you freshly baked cookies, they treat you like family and they're the one you hope is in charge of bringing the main dish to the potluck. After nearly a decade in the blogosphere, Leigh Anne is now veritably the favorite neighbor to thousands who come to her site daily to search the more than 2,400 delicious, easy recipes and Pinterest-worthy ideas for entertaining.

Leigh Anne firmly believes in eating dinner together as a family, having done so as a child and when raising children of her own. She's cultivated an online space for parents to find and make simple, straightforward and picky eater–proof recipes.

Leigh Anne is also a mother of four amazing grown children and a mother-in-law to two beautiful daughters-in-law who she is grateful for daily. Leigh Anne and her husband, Jim, live in Portland, Oregon. They've been married for more than 35 years and are adjusting to life as empty nesters.

She loves feeding people, throwing parties, burying her head in a book and digging in the dirt in her garden. Her husband would tell you she loves making messes and finding junk (treasures) at Goodwill. She lives by the mantra taped to her fridge: "Love people, and make them good food." She's designed this cookbook to help you do the same.

INDEX